NETWORKING SUCCESS

How to be the First Person Selected for Any Opportunity

WRITTEN BY:

MICHELLE DORNOR

COPYRIGHT

Copyright©2023 Dornor Consulting LLC

All rights reserved. No part of this book may be reproduced or transmitted in any form or by any means, electronic or mechanical, including photocopying, recording or by any information storage and retrieval system, without written permission from the author, except for the inclusion of brief quotations in a review.

Printed in the United States of America

First Printing, 2023

Special Edition, Networking Success Masterclass 2023

Dornor Consulting Publishing

Cheyenne, Wyoming

www.dornorconsulting.com

All images/photographs are author's personal photos except where notated free use via Pexels.com & may not be used without prior written consent from publisher & author.

Dedication

Why I wrote this book

I wrote this book to bring awareness to the power of effective networking. Most people do not spend enough time learning about networking because they do not get instant gratification. Networking is like creating a fine dining experience. It is not rushed as relationships built right over time produce prosperous results. I want to share my knowledge, wisdom, and personal experience with those who are looking for guidance or need a refresher in the basics of networking with other people successfully.

MY ASK

My hope is that the words contained herein will encourage your spirit to pursue your highest good and purpose. If the words herein have touched you in some way please leave a positive review & share on your social media pages with the hashtag:

#networkingsuccess

With Love, Michelle

NETWORKING SUCCESS

TABLE OF CONTENTS

Copyright	2
Dedication	3
The Negatives	7
The Positives	10
Definitions	25
Computers and People	31
The Proof Networking Works	39
Networking and Your Body	42
Efficiencies and Deficiencies	48
The Reason Most People Fail	54
Overcoming the Fears	62
Personality Types	70
The Principles of Networking	90
The Rules of Engagement	96
How to Create a Strong Network	101
Working the Room	104
Step by Step Approach	108
Additional Tips and Tricks	114
Going Global	118
Resources	128
Key Takeaways	131
Sayings & Quotes	134
Affirmations & Mantras	138

Welcome to Networking Success Masterclass!

Are you unsure of how to capture the attention of the right people that can give you access to the right opportunities?

Are you an introvert and need guidance in how to increase your visibility?

Do you want to be top of mind when people are discussing new projects and positions?

If you answered yes to any of the above, then this class and the accompanying workbook is for you! Even if have some of the networking basics down, we can always use some reminding of what does and doesn't work.

Why is it important to know how to network properly? Everyone has heard of the saying "Your network is your net worth". Well, its true! The way you interact and build relationships will largely determine your ability to rise to higher heights. No matter what business you are in, you are in the people business. This class is going to show you how to navigate the art of building successful relationships with others through networking.

Let's discover some reasons why it is important to network properly for success.

Negative outcomes from networking improperly:

Wasted time and energy

Wasted time hiring the wrong people over and over

Negative Personal and Professional brand

Lack of Influence

Loss of Credibility, Trust, and Reputation

Lack of a Supportive Network

Lack of the right kind of guidance

Missed opportunities

Limited Exposure and Limited Access to the right people places and things

Hindered personal and professional growth and development

As we can see from the possible negative outcomes above, networking improperly can not only be damaging financially, it can also damage your reputation if done incorrectly. This class and workbook is going to teach you how to network for success.

Everyone can benefit from networking with success! No matter what business you are in, you are in the people business.

Business Owners & Entrepreneurs!

Save thousands in recruiting the right people the first time!

Increase your problem-solving abilities!

Stay Informed on the latest trends, insights, and emerging business opportunities!

Establish your business as the Thought Leader in your industry!

Drive positive change and engagement by gaining access to diverse perspectives & best practices!

Tap into a broader pool of the right type of candidates and save thousands in recruiting efforts for your business!

Increase your revenue by partnering with the right professional

Gain access to diverse perspectives exposed by being in the right circles to expand on problem solving abilities!

Professionals and Career People!

"Get Tapped on the Shoulder" for more opportunities for Advancement

Negotiate better pay, raises, positions, & promotions for yourself

Gain Access to the best mentors for faster learning to reach your goals quickly

Leverage new connections for personal growth and development

Increase Access to Profitable Collaborations

Build lasting Relationships that Pay in more ways then one!

Increase your visibility & Credibility

Build a positive personal brand & reputation

Gain Access to "Insider Information" thru the right connections

Develop strong confidence and speaking ability

Homemakers & Community Leaders!

Get your ideas in front of the right people

Stop wasting time & money making the wrong connections

Build a positive personal brand & reputation

Foster stronger bonds & relationships

As you can see from the preceding lists, no matter what station in life you may find yourself, you are indeed in the people business! Let us dive deeper into this material on networking success and see how we can create win-win situations in our relationship with others.

The positive outcomes of networking

Networking successfully with the right people can lead to a variety of positive outcomes. Here are some possible outcomes that can result from effective networking:

1. **Increased Opportunities**: Networking can open doors to new opportunities, such as job offers, business partnerships, or collaborations. By connecting with the right people, you may discover new projects, career advancements, or ventures that align with your goals and aspirations.

2. **Access to Knowledge and Resources**: Building a strong network allows you to tap into a vast pool of knowledge, expertise, and resources. You can gain valuable insights, learn from the experiences of others, and access industry-specific information that can help you make informed decisions and stay ahead in your field.

3. **Expanded Professional Circle**: Networking enables you to expand your professional circle and connect with individuals from diverse backgrounds and industries. This can lead to a broader perspective, exposure to different ideas, and the opportunity to forge meaningful relationships with people who can offer support, guidance, and mentorship.

4. **Enhanced Visibility and Reputation**: By networking effectively, you can raise your visibility within your industry or professional community. Engaging with influential individuals and thought leaders can help you establish a positive reputation and increase your credibility. This can lead to recognition, invitations to speak at events, or being sought after for collaborations or partnerships.

5. **Personal and Professional Growth**: Networking provides opportunities for personal and professional growth. Engaging with others allows you to develop and refine your communication, interpersonal, and relationship-building skills. Through networking, you can gain confidence, broaden your perspectives, and learn from the experiences and insights of others.

6. **Supportive Community**: Building a strong network can create a supportive community of like-minded individuals who share similar interests, challenges, and aspirations. This community can offer encouragement, advice, and emotional support. Networking events and communities can serve as platforms for

exchanging ideas, celebrating successes, and finding solutions to common problems.

7. **Referrals and Recommendations**: By establishing trusted relationships through networking, you increase the likelihood of receiving referrals and recommendations. When people in your network understand your skills, expertise, and values, they are more likely to refer you to opportunities or recommend your services to their connections.

8. **Collaboration and Partnerships**: Networking can lead to valuable collaborations and partnerships. By connecting with individuals who complement your skills and areas of expertise, you can form synergistic partnerships that lead to innovative projects, joint ventures, or shared initiatives. Collaboration with the right people can amplify your impact and expand your reach.

9. **Long-Term Friendships**: Networking goes beyond professional connections; it can also foster long-term friendships. Through shared interests, experiences, and goals, networking can create lasting bonds with individuals who become trusted friends, confidants, and supporters throughout your personal and professional journey.

10. **Continuous Learning and Development**: Engaging with a diverse network allows for continuous learning and development. Through conversations, discussions, and sharing of insights, you can stay updated with industry trends, gain new knowledge, and refine your skills. Networking provides a platform for ongoing education and self-improvement.

11. **Industry Influence and Thought Leadership**: Networking with influential individuals in your industry can help you establish yourself as a thought leader. By actively participating in discussions, sharing valuable insights, and contributing to industry events or publications, you can position yourself as an expert and gain influence within your field.

12. **Access to Funding or Investment Opportunities**: Effective networking can connect you with potential investors, venture capitalists, or funding sources for your business or projects. Building relationships with individuals in the finance or investment sector can open doors to funding opportunities, mentorship, or partnerships that support your professional endeavors.

13. **Business Growth and Client Acquisition**: Networking can lead to business growth by connecting you with potential clients, customers, or strategic partners. By building relationships with decision-makers and key stakeholders in your target market, you increase the chances of securing new business opportunities and expanding your customer base.

14. **Industry Insights and Market Trends**: Engaging with a diverse network allows you to stay informed about industry insights, market trends, and emerging opportunities. Through conversations, conferences, and networking events, you can gain valuable market intelligence that helps you adapt, innovate, and stay ahead of the competition.

15. **Professional Development and Skill Enhancement**: Networking can provide opportunities for professional development and skill enhancement. Engaging with individuals who possess expertise or knowledge in areas you want to develop can lead to mentorship, training, or guidance. By leveraging your network, you can access learning opportunities and resources that contribute to your growth.

16. **Cross-Cultural and Global Connections**: Networking with individuals from different cultural backgrounds or geographic locations can broaden your perspectives and expand your global reach. Building cross-cultural connections enables you to learn from diverse perspectives, establish international collaborations, and tap into new markets or opportunities beyond your immediate network.

17. **Social Impact and Giving Back**: Networking can extend beyond personal and professional gains. By connecting with individuals who share a passion for social impact, sustainability, or philanthropy, you can contribute to meaningful causes and make a difference in your community. Networking can facilitate partnerships for social initiatives or support projects aligned with your values.

18. **Confidence and Personal Empowerment**: Successful networking can boost your confidence and enhance your sense of personal empowerment. As you build connections, receive positive feedback, and witness the positive impact of your networking efforts, you develop a stronger belief in your abilities and potential, which can have a profound impact on your overall success and well-being.

19. **Mentorship and Guidance**: Through networking, you may find mentors or experienced professionals who can provide guidance and advice based on their

own experiences. These mentors can offer valuable insights, help you navigate challenges, and provide support as you progress in your career or business endeavors.

20. **Increased Confidence in Social Settings**: Networking frequently allows you to become more comfortable and confident in social settings. By engaging in conversations, practicing active listening, and building connections, you develop stronger social skills that can benefit you not only in professional networking but also in various social situations.

21. **Career Advancement Opportunities**: Effective networking can lead to career advancement opportunities such as promotions, job offers, or career transitions. By connecting with influential individuals within your industry, you increase your visibility and become more likely to be considered for exciting professional opportunities.

22. **Access to Insider Information**: Building relationships with individuals in key positions can grant you access to valuable insider information within your industry. This knowledge can include upcoming trends, emerging technologies, or market insights that give you a competitive edge and help you stay ahead of the curve.

23. **Collaborative Projects and Innovation**: Networking can result in collaborative projects or partnerships that drive innovation. By connecting with individuals who possess complementary skills and expertise, you can form teams that bring diverse perspectives to problem-solving and spark innovation through collective creativity.

24. **Brand Building and Personal Reputation**: Successfully networking with the right people can enhance your personal brand and reputation. Through positive interactions, delivering on commitments, and adding value to your network, you build a strong professional reputation that opens doors to new opportunities and garners respect within your industry.

25. **Access to Exclusive Events and Conferences**: Networking can provide access to exclusive events, conferences, or industry gatherings. These gatherings often attract influential speakers, thought leaders, and industry experts. Attending such events enables you to expand your network further, learn from renowned professionals, and stay up to date with the latest trends and insights.

26. **Cross-Industry Connections**: Networking can introduce you to professionals from diverse industries, allowing you to explore cross-industry collaborations and leverage knowledge and practices from other sectors. These connections can lead to fresh perspectives, new business ideas, and the ability to apply innovative approaches to your own field.

27. **Professional Validation and Recognition**: By networking successfully, you gain recognition and validation from peers, colleagues, and industry experts. This validation can boost your confidence, affirm your expertise, and open doors to speaking engagements, panel discussions, or thought leadership opportunities where you can share your knowledge and insights.

28. **Access to Industry Trends and Forecasting**: Networking can provide valuable insights into industry trends, market shifts, and future developments. By connecting with individuals who are knowledgeable about your industry, you can gain access to information that helps you anticipate changes, adapt your strategies, and stay ahead of the competition.

29. **Personal and Professional Empowerment**: Successful networking can empower you personally and professionally. Through meaningful connections, you can gain a sense of belonging, inspiration, and motivation. Networking allows you to surround yourself with like-minded individuals who share your drive for success, helping you stay focused and motivated on your journey.

30. **Cultural and Diversity Understanding**: Networking with individuals from diverse backgrounds offers the opportunity to broaden your cultural understanding and develop a more inclusive mindset. By engaging with people of different ethnicities, nationalities, and perspectives, you expand your worldview and enhance your cultural intelligence, which is valuable in an increasingly globalized society.

31. **Community Building and Social Impact**: Effective networking can lead to community building and social impact. By connecting with individuals who are passionate about making a positive difference, you can collaborate on community projects, engage in philanthropic initiatives, or contribute to causes that align with your values. Networking can amplify your collective impact and create lasting change.

32. **Emotional Support and Well-being**: Networking can provide emotional support and a sense of belonging. Building a supportive network of individuals

who understand and empathize with your professional challenges and successes can positively impact your well-being. By sharing experiences, seeking advice, and offering support, you create a network that nurtures your mental and emotional health.

33. **Lifelong Learning and Continued Growth**: Engaging with the right people through networking allows for continuous learning and growth. By staying connected with industry leaders, attending seminars, webinars, or workshops, and participating in industry-related discussions, you expand your knowledge, stay updated with the latest trends, and foster a growth mindset.

34. **Intercultural Collaboration and Global Opportunities**: Networking with individuals from different countries and cultures presents opportunities for intercultural collaboration and global partnerships. By building relationships with professionals worldwide, you can explore international markets, exchange ideas, and leverage cross-cultural expertise to expand your reach and impact.

35. **Mentorship and Paying It Forward**: As you advance in your career and expand your network, you can pay it forward by becoming a mentor to others.

36. **Industry Insights and Best Practices**: Through networking, you gain access to industry insights, best practices, and insider knowledge. By connecting with experienced professionals, thought leaders, and influencers, you can learn from their expertise, gain valuable tips, and stay updated on the latest industry trends and strategies.

37. **Professional Recognition and Awards**: Effective networking can increase your visibility and enhance your chances of receiving professional recognition and awards. As you build relationships and establish a positive reputation within your industry, you become more likely to be nominated for accolades, industry-specific awards, or speaking opportunities at prestigious events.

38. **Industry Collaboration and Advocacy**: Networking can foster collaboration and advocacy within your industry. By connecting with professionals who share similar goals and values, you can collectively work towards common objectives, advocate for industry improvements, and drive positive change. Networking enables you to find like-minded individuals and build a united front to address industry challenges.

39. **Access to Training and Development Opportunities**: Building a strong network can provide access to training programs, workshops, or development opportunities that enhance your skills and knowledge. Through connections with training providers, industry associations, or mentors, you can access resources and programs that support your professional growth and continuous development.

40. **Business and Investment Opportunities**: Successful networking can lead to business and investment opportunities. By building relationships with entrepreneurs, investors, or business owners, you increase your chances of discovering potential partnerships, funding opportunities, or even investment prospects for your own ventures.

41. **Enhanced Problem-Solving Abilities**: Networking exposes you to diverse perspectives and solutions to common challenges. By engaging with individuals from different industries, backgrounds, and expertise, you expand your problem-solving abilities. Through collaboration and brainstorming, you can uncover innovative approaches to address complex issues and find creative solutions.

42. **Recruitment and Talent Acquisition**: Networking provides opportunities for talent acquisition and recruitment. By connecting with professionals in your field, you can tap into a pool of potential candidates for job openings within your organization. Leveraging your network allows you to identify top talent, build relationships with potential hires, and access a broader talent pool.

43. **Personal and Professional Balance**: Effective networking can contribute to achieving a balance between personal and professional life. By connecting with individuals who prioritize work-life integration, well-being, and personal growth, you can gain insights and strategies to maintain a healthy balance, manage stress, and enhance overall life satisfaction.

44. **Cross-Generational Connections**: Networking enables cross-generational connections that bridge the gap between different age groups. By engaging with professionals from different generations, you can learn from their experiences, perspectives, and wisdom. These intergenerational connections foster mutual learning and mentorship opportunities that can accelerate personal and professional growth.

The outcomes of networking are not always immediate or guaranteed. Building a strong network requires consistent effort, genuine engagement, and nurturing relationships over time. It's essential to approach networking with a long-term mindset, focusing on building authentic connections and adding value to others. Through patience, perseverance, and a proactive approach, you can maximize the outcomes of successful networking and create a positive impact on your personal and professional journey.

Successful networking outcomes are multifaceted and can vary based on individual goals, industry, and the specific connections made. It's important to approach networking with an open mind, genuine interest in others, and a willingness to contribute and add value to your network. By nurturing relationships, staying connected, and seizing opportunities, you can experience a wide range of positive outcomes that contribute to your long-term success and fulfillment.

Networking is a continual process that requires ongoing effort, sincerity, and a willingness to build and maintain relationships. The benefits and outcomes you experience may vary based on your individual circumstances and the specific connections you make. Stay open-minded, be proactive, and embrace the possibilities that effective networking can bring to your personal and professional life. By doing so, you increase the likelihood of experiencing these positive outcomes and unlocking new opportunities for personal and professional growth.

The Negative Outcomes of Ineffective Networking

Networking unsuccessfully with the wrong people can have various outcomes that may not be as beneficial or desirable. Here are some possible outcomes from networking unsuccessfully with the wrong people:

1. **Wasted Time and Energy**: Connecting with the wrong people can result in wasted time and energy. Engaging in conversations or interactions that do not align with your goals or values can drain your resources and divert your focus away from more meaningful connections.

2. **Missed Opportunities**: Networking with individuals who do not share your interests, industry, or professional goals can lead to missed opportunities. By investing time in connections that do not align with your objectives, you may overlook or miss out on potential collaborations, job openings, or valuable insights that could have advanced your career or business.

3. **Lack of Relevance and Value**: Networking with individuals who are not relevant to your field or industry may result in a lack of value in the conversations or interactions. The information exchanged may not be applicable or beneficial to your professional growth or endeavors, limiting the learning and knowledge-sharing opportunities.

4. **Negative Reputation or Associations**: Associating with the wrong people can impact your reputation negatively. If you are seen engaging with individuals who have a poor professional reputation or are involved in unethical practices, it can reflect poorly on your own credibility and integrity.

5. **Loss of Trust and Credibility**: Networking with the wrong people can erode trust and credibility within your network. By associating with individuals known for unethical behavior, dishonesty, or lack of professionalism, others may question your judgment and integrity, leading to a loss of trust and potential opportunities.

6. **Distraction from Goals**: Networking with the wrong people can divert your attention from your goals and priorities. Engaging in superficial or unproductive conversations can lead to a lack of focus on your own personal or professional development, hindering your progress and growth.

NETWORKING SUCCESS

7. **Misaligned Connections**: Networking with individuals who do not share your values, work ethic, or vision can result in misaligned connections. These connections may not provide the support, mentorship, or guidance that you seek, leaving you without the necessary resources or guidance to advance in your career or business.

8. **Negative Influence and Impact**: Associating with the wrong people can expose you to negative influences and behaviors. If you surround yourself with individuals who have a pessimistic or defeatist mindset, it can affect your own motivation, confidence, and outlook on success.

9. **Drained Motivation and Enthusiasm**: Networking with individuals who do not share your passion or drive can drain your motivation and enthusiasm. Interactions that lack inspiration or engagement may dampen your own ambition and hinder your ability to stay motivated and pursue your goals.

10. **Missed Learning Opportunities**: Networking unsuccessfully with the wrong people can result in missed learning opportunities. By not engaging with individuals who can offer valuable insights, diverse perspectives, or industry-specific knowledge, you may limit your own growth and miss out on new ideas or approaches.

11. **Lack of Support and Guidance**: Networking with the wrong people may result in a lack of support and guidance. If the individuals you connect with are not interested in helping or mentoring others, you may find yourself without the support system necessary to navigate challenges or seek advice when needed.

12. **Negative Influence on Personal Brand**: Associating with the wrong people can have a negative impact on your personal brand. If you are consistently seen with individuals who have a poor reputation or engage in unprofessional behavior, it can tarnish your own image and credibility in the eyes of others.

13. **Missed Collaborative Opportunities**: Networking with individuals who are not collaborative or open to partnerships can lead to missed collaborative opportunities. Building successful collaborations requires a level of mutual trust, shared goals, and complementary skills. Connecting with individuals who are not interested in collaboration can limit your ability to embark on joint ventures or leverage collective strengths.

14. **Limited Access to Resources**: Networking with the wrong people may result in limited access to valuable resources. Connections with individuals who do not have a wide network or access to industry-specific resources can restrict your own access to information, funding, or opportunities that could propel your success.

15. **Emotional Exhaustion**: Engaging with the wrong people can be emotionally draining. If the individuals you network with are negative, unsupportive, or constantly bring you down, it can have a detrimental effect on your motivation, enthusiasm, and overall well-being.

16. **Hindered Professional Growth**: Networking with individuals who do not challenge or inspire you can hinder your professional growth. Surrounding yourself with individuals who do not push you to improve, learn, or expand your skill set can limit your own development and hinder your ability to reach new heights in your career.

17. **Limited Diversity of Perspectives**: Networking with the wrong people can result in a limited diversity of perspectives. Connecting with individuals who come from similar backgrounds or have similar experiences may restrict your exposure to new ideas, innovative thinking, and fresh approaches to problem-solving.

18. **Missed Personal Connections**: Networking unsuccessfully with the wrong people may mean missing out on establishing meaningful personal connections. Building a strong network goes beyond professional gains. It also involves forming genuine connections and friendships with individuals who share common interests, values, and experiences.

19. **Decreased Confidence and Self-Esteem**: Consistently interacting with the wrong people, who may belittle your ambitions or undermine your abilities, can negatively impact your confidence and self-esteem. Surrounding yourself with individuals who do not support your goals or believe in your potential can erode your self-confidence and hinder your personal growth.

20. **Lack of Inspiration and Motivation**: Networking with individuals who do not inspire or motivate you can leave you feeling stagnant or uninspired. Connecting with people who lack ambition, drive, or a positive outlook on success may diminish your own motivation and hinder your ability to strive for excellence.

21. **Decreased Trust in Networking**: Networking with the wrong people can result in a decreased trust in the networking process as a whole. Negative

experiences or interactions with individuals who are unprofessional, insincere, or disinterested can erode your faith in the power of networking and its potential benefits.

22. **Lack of Synergy and Collaboration**: Networking with individuals who do not share your values, vision, or work style can lead to a lack of synergy and collaboration. Building successful collaborations requires a level of alignment and mutual understanding, and connecting with individuals who are not compatible with your goals or work approach can hinder your ability to form productive partnerships.

23. **Missed Learning and Skill Development Opportunities**: Networking unsuccessfully with the wrong people may mean missing out on valuable learning and skill development opportunities. Engaging with individuals who do not offer valuable insights, industry knowledge, or unique perspectives can limit your ability to learn and grow within your professional field.

24. **Ineffectiveness in Building a Supportive Network**: Networking with the wrong people can make it difficult to build a supportive network. If the individuals you connect with are not interested in supporting or advocating for others, you may struggle to find the support and encouragement needed to overcome challenges and achieve your goals.

25. **Emotional Disconnection**: Networking unsuccessfully with the wrong people may lead to emotional disconnection. If your interactions lack authenticity, genuine interest, or meaningful connections, you may feel disconnected or isolated within your networking circles, making it challenging to establish long-lasting relationships.

26. **Limited Exposure to Opportunities**: Networking with individuals who do not have access to a diverse range of opportunities can limit your exposure to new ventures, projects, or career advancements. Connecting with individuals who are not well-connected or influential within their industries may restrict your access to a broader range of opportunities.

27. **Negative Impact on Motivation and Ambition**: Consistently interacting with individuals who lack motivation, ambition, or a growth mindset can negatively impact your own motivation and ambition. Being surrounded by individuals who do not strive for excellence or seek continuous improvement can hinder your own drive to succeed and reach your full potential.

28. **Stagnation and Limited Growth**: Networking unsuccessfully with the wrong people can result in stagnation and limited professional growth. If the individuals you connect with do not challenge or inspire you, you may find yourself in a comfort zone that inhibits your ability to take risks, seek new opportunities, and embrace personal and professional growth.

29. **Decreased Confidence in Networking Skills**: Continuous networking with the wrong people can erode your confidence in your networking skills. Negative experiences or lack of positive outcomes may make you doubt your ability to effectively connect with others, resulting in hesitancy or reluctance to engage in future networking opportunities.

30. **Diminished Networking Reputation**: Networking with individuals who have a negative reputation or lack professionalism can impact your own networking reputation. Associating with individuals who are known for unethical behavior, unreliability, or poor communication skills can reflect poorly on your own credibility and hinder your ability to build meaningful connections with others.

31. **Missed Industry Insights and Trends**: Networking with individuals who are not well-informed or connected within your industry can result in missed insights and trends. These individuals may not be able to provide you with valuable industry knowledge, updates, or insider information that can help you stay informed and adapt to changing market dynamics.

32. **Hindered Personal and Professional Development**: Networking unsuccessfully with the wrong people can hinder your personal and professional development. If the individuals you connect with do not offer mentorship, guidance, or constructive feedback, you may miss out on opportunities to improve your skills, expand your knowledge, and grow as a professional.

33. **Limited Access to Referrals and Recommendations**: Building a network with the wrong people can limit your access to referrals and recommendations. These individuals may not be inclined to recommend your services or connect you with potential clients, customers, or job opportunities, reducing your chances of expanding your business or advancing in your career.

34. **Negative Impact on Work-Life Balance**: Networking with individuals who do not prioritize work-life balance or share similar values can negatively impact your own work-life balance. If the people in your network constantly promote a

work-centric lifestyle or disregard the importance of personal well-being, it can influence your own perception of work-life balance and hinder your ability to achieve harmony in your life.

35. **Frustration and Disappointment**: Continuously networking with the wrong people can lead to frustration and disappointment. If your interactions lack substance, meaningful connections, or genuine interest, it can leave you feeling dissatisfied with the networking process and questioning its effectiveness in achieving your goals.

36. **Limited Access to Supportive Communities**: Networking with individuals who are not interested in building supportive communities can hinder your ability to access a network of like-minded individuals. These individuals may not be willing to offer support, advice, or a sense of community, leaving you without a strong network to lean on during challenging times or celebrate successes with.

37. **Missed Opportunities for Collaboration and Innovation**: Networking unsuccessfully with the wrong people may mean missing out on collaboration and innovation opportunities. Connecting with individuals who are not open to collaboration, brainstorming, or sharing ideas can limit your ability to explore new possibilities, pool resources, and engage in creative problem-solving.

38. **Decreased Motivation and Enthusiasm**: Networking with individuals who lack motivation, enthusiasm, or a positive outlook can diminish your own motivation and enthusiasm. Surrounding yourself with individuals who are not passionate or driven can dampen your own ambition and hinder your ability to maintain high levels of motivation in pursuing your goals.

39. **Limited Exposure to Diverse Perspectives**: Networking with the wrong people can restrict your exposure to diverse perspectives and ideas. Connecting with individuals who come from similar backgrounds or have similar experiences may limit your ability to broaden your horizons, challenge your own assumptions, and gain fresh insights from different viewpoints.

40. **Detrimental Impact on Well-being**: Networking unsuccessfully with the wrong people can have a detrimental impact on your overall well-being. Negative interactions, toxic relationships, or constant exposure to individuals who drain your energy can lead to stress, anxiety, and a negative mindset that can affect both your personal and professional life.

It's important to approach networking with intentionality and discernment. Be selective in building connections with individuals who share similar values, goals, and a growth mindset. By surrounding yourself with the right people, you can enhance your networking experience and maximize the positive outcomes that contribute to your personal and professional success.

It's essential to reflect on your networking experiences and learn from them. Recognize the importance of being selective with the individuals you choose to network with, seeking those who align with your values, goals, and professional aspirations. By being intentional about your networking efforts and surrounding yourself with the right people, you can maximize the positive outcomes and create a strong network that supports your personal and professional growth.

It's crucial to evaluate and choose your networking connections wisely to ensure that they align with your goals, values, and aspirations. By surrounding yourself with individuals who support, challenge, and inspire you, you increase the likelihood of positive outcomes and maximize the benefits of networking.

Definitions of Network & Net Worth

The terms "network" and "net worth" have distinct etymologies and origins. Let's delve into their etymological backgrounds:

Network:
The word "network" derives from the combination of two Old English words: "net" and "weorc" (meaning "work"). In Old English, the term "net" referred to a woven mesh of threads used for catching fish or trapping game. Over time, "net" evolved to encompass the broader concept of interconnected threads or lines.

The term "network" emerged in the mid-16th century and originally referred to a system of interconnected threads or cords used for various purposes. By the late 17th century, it took on a metaphorical sense, referring to a complex interconnected system or structure.

The modern understanding of "network" emerged in the mid-20th century with the rise of telecommunication and computing. It came to represent a system of interconnected nodes, such as computers, devices, or people, facilitating communication, information exchange, and collaboration.

History of the word "net":

The word "net" has a long history, dating back to Old English and beyond. It can be traced back to the Proto-Germanic word "*natją," which meant "net" or "mesh." This term further evolved from the Proto-Indo-European root "*ned-," which conveys the idea of binding or tying.

In Old English, the word for "net" was "nett," referring to a woven mesh of threads or cords used for catching fish or trapping game. The Old English word "nett" gave rise to the Middle English term "nette" and eventually to the modern English word "net."

Sanskrit equivalent of the word "net":

In Sanskrit, the term for "net" is "jaalam" (जालम्), derived from the Sanskrit root "jāl" (जाल), which means "to entwine" or "to catch in a net." The word "jaalam" encompasses the idea of a woven structure used for trapping or catching.

Sanskrit is an ancient Indo-Aryan language and has a rich vocabulary related to various aspects of life. The Sanskrit term "jaalam" is used to describe a net or a network-like structure that is used for various purposes, including catching fish, trapping animals, or even metaphorically referring to interconnected systems.

History of the word "work":

The word "work" traces its origins back to Old English and has Germanic roots. It is derived from the Old English word "weorc," which denoted a wide range of activities involving physical or mental effort, labor, or action.

The Old English term "weorc" has cognates in other Germanic languages, such as the Old High German "werc" and the Old Norse "verk." These words share a common Proto-Germanic origin, "*werkaną," which conveys the sense of working or laboring.

Sanskrit equivalent of the word "work":

In Sanskrit, the term for "work" is "karma" (कर्म), derived from the Sanskrit root "kar" (कर्), which means "to do" or "to act." The word "karma" encompasses the broader concept of action, duty, or the consequences of one's actions.

In the ancient Indian philosophy of Hinduism and Buddhism, "karma" holds a significant meaning. It refers to the sum total of an individual's actions and the moral or ethical consequences that result from those actions.

Sanskrit literature, including texts such as the Bhagavad Gita, extensively discusses the concept of "karma" and its implications on personal and spiritual growth.

In summary, the word "net" has its roots in Old English and Proto-Germanic, while its Sanskrit equivalent is "jaalam." The term "work" also originates from Old English and Proto-Germanic, while its Sanskrit counterpart is "karma." Both English and Sanskrit words have a long history and rich cultural associations, reflecting the human activities of capturing, connecting, and undertaking actions.

Sanskrit equivalent of the word "net" (alternative term):

In addition to "jaalam," another Sanskrit term for "net" is "sutra" (सूत्र). Derived from the Sanskrit root "siv" (सिव्), meaning "to sew" or "to string together," "sutra" refers to a thread or cord used for tying or binding. It also represents a string or thread woven into a net-like structure.

"Sutra" holds significant importance in various contexts, including the ancient Indian scriptures known as the Sutras, which are concise aphoristic statements or teachings on different subjects. These teachings are presented in a structured and interconnected manner, resembling a net of knowledge.

Sanskrit equivalent of the word "work" (alternative term):

Apart from "karma," another Sanskrit term for "work" is "kriya" (क्रिया). Derived from the Sanskrit root "kri" (क्री), meaning "to do," "kriya" represents action, activity, or performance. It refers to any form of work or action carried out with intention and purpose.

In Sanskrit grammar, "kriya" also refers to the verbal actions or processes expressed by verbs. It encompasses the idea of doing, performing, or accomplishing.

The concept of "kriya" is deeply rooted in Hindu philosophy, particularly in the branch of Yoga known as Karma Yoga, which emphasizes selfless action performed with detachment from the outcomes.

Sanskrit philosophical concept of interconnectedness:

Sanskrit philosophical and spiritual traditions emphasize the interconnectedness of all things, which aligns with the idea of networking or interconnectivity. In Sanskrit, the term "sambandha" (संबन्ध) represents the concept of interconnectedness, relationships, or connections.

"Sambandha" encompasses the understanding that everything in the universe is interconnected and influences each other. It reflects the notion of a network of relationships that exists at various levels, whether between individuals, ideas, or cosmic elements.

This philosophical perspective of interconnectedness in Sanskrit contributes to a broader understanding of the significance of networks and connections in various realms of life.

Sanskrit offers alternative terms for both "net" ("jaalam" and "sutra") and "work" ("karma" and "kriya"). These Sanskrit terms deepen our exploration of the concepts of interconnectedness, action, and the weaving of networks. Sanskrit, with its profound philosophical traditions, provides valuable insights into the cultural, linguistic, and spiritual dimensions related to these words.

So what we can determine from the above definitions and etymology of network is that it is a string of actions that ties directly back to your life and your daily routine. Your daily routine includes people. You have to be connected to a string of people that will ultimately help you reach your desired goal.

Let me ask you a question. What is your goal? Are the people you are tied to able to help you somehow reach that goal?

Let's move on to the definition of net worth.

Net Worth:

The term "net worth" has a more recent origin and is closely associated with financial and economic contexts. It refers to the value of a person's or entity's assets minus its liabilities, representing their overall financial standing.

The word "net" in "net worth" is derived from the Old English "nett," which referred to a woven fabric or mesh used for various purposes. It eventually extended to include the meaning of "final" or "remaining" after deductions.

The concept of "net worth" as a financial term gained prominence in the early 20th century. It reflects the idea of calculating an individual's or organization's true financial position by subtracting liabilities or debts from their total assets. The term is widely used in business, finance, and personal finance to assess an entity's financial health and wealth.

It's worth noting that while "network" and "net worth" share the common root word "net," their etymological paths diverge, with "network" focusing on interconnected systems and "net worth" centering on financial valuation.

The term "network" originated from Old English words for woven mesh or cords, evolving to represent interconnected systems, while "net worth" emerged in the context of financial assessment, deriving from the concept of final or remaining value after deductions.

The term "worth" has its roots in Old English and can be traced back to the Proto-Germanic language. The word "worth" comes from the Old English word "weorþ," which meant "value," "price," or "worthiness."

In turn, "weorþ" can be traced back to the Proto-Germanic word "*werþaz," which had a similar meaning of "value" or "worth." This Proto-Germanic root also gave rise to related words in other Germanic languages, such as the Old High German "werda" and the Old Norse "verðr."

The concept of "worth" has been associated with evaluating the value or quality of something. It refers to the significance, importance, or desirability of an object, idea, or individual. "Worth" is often used to describe the monetary or material value of something, but it can also encompass broader aspects such as moral or personal value.

Over time, the word "worth" has retained its essential meaning while adapting to changes in language and usage. It has become an integral part of the English language, used in various contexts to express value, worthiness, or significance.

The etymology of the word "worth" extends beyond the Old English and Proto-Germanic roots to include influences from other languages, including Sanskrit.

In Sanskrit, an ancient Indo-Aryan language, the term "vṛddhi" (वृद्धि) is closely related to the concept of worth or value. "Vṛddhi" is derived from the Sanskrit root "vṛdh" (वृध्), which means "to grow" or "to increase." In Sanskrit grammar, the term "vṛddhi" refers to the augmenting or elongation of a vowel sound.

The connection between the Sanskrit "vṛddhi" and the English "worth" lies in their shared idea of growth or increase. In both languages, the concept of worth involves the idea of something gaining value or becoming more significant.

Sanskrit equivalent of the word "worth":

The Sanskrit term for "worth" is "artha" (अर्थ). Derived from the Sanskrit root "ṛt" (ऋत्), which means "to prosper," "artha" encompasses the concepts of value, meaning, purpose, wealth, and significance.

In Sanskrit philosophy, "artha" represents one of the four goals of human life, known as "purusharthas." These goals include dharma (duty/righteousness), artha (material wealth/prosperity), kama (pleasure/desire), and moksha (liberation/spiritual realization). "Artha" denotes the pursuit of material wealth and prosperity as an essential aspect of human life.

Additionally, the Sanskrit word "arthavat" (अर्थवत्) implies "having worth" or "being meaningful" and is derived from the same root. It signifies something that holds value, significance, or purpose.

Philosophical dimensions of worth in Sanskrit:

In Sanskrit philosophical traditions, the concept of "worth" extends beyond material possessions and encompasses broader dimensions of value and significance. It explores the intrinsic worth or inherent value of individuals and objects beyond their utilitarian or economic value.

Sanskrit philosophical texts, such as the Upanishads and the Vedas, delve into the nature of existence, reality, and the purpose of life. They examine the worth or intrinsic value of the self (Atman) and the ultimate reality (Brahman).

The idea of worth in Sanskrit philosophy connects with the concept of "Sat-Chit-Ananda," representing truth, consciousness, and bliss. It reflects the understanding that true worth lies in the realization of one's innate nature and the recognition of the interconnectedness of all beings.

Linguistic influence of Sanskrit on the word "worth":

While the specific etymological influence of Sanskrit on the English word "worth" may not be directly traceable, Sanskrit has significantly influenced the development of various Indo-European languages, including English.

Through linguistic and cultural exchanges, Sanskrit has enriched the vocabulary and concepts of other languages. The shared Indo-European linguistic heritage suggests that Sanskrit may have contributed to shaping the understanding and expression of worth in English and related languages.

The etymology of the word "worth" can be traced back to Old English and Proto-Germanic roots, reflecting the concept of value, price, or worthiness. Today, "worth" remains a fundamental term for evaluating the value and importance of things and individuals.

The Sanskrit equivalent of the word "worth" is "artha," encompassing the ideas of value, meaning, purpose, and material prosperity. Sanskrit philosophical traditions explore the broader dimensions of worth, emphasizing intrinsic value, interconnectedness, and the pursuit of spiritual realization. While the specific influence of Sanskrit on the English word "worth" may not be directly traceable, the deep philosophical insights of Sanskrit contribute to a broader understanding of the concept of worth in different dimensions of life.

Tying back what we just discovered about the meaning of net worth is based on the value of our relationship with other people or things. Which side of the balance sheet are your relationships, left or right? Are they liabilities or assets? Do those relationships increase or decrease your value and worthiness in the social world?

People and Computers

Now we are going to discuss the principles of networking and how they are closely related to computer networking. Most people do not know that the first computer was actually a human. Let show you.

Computer
1640s, "one who calculates, a reckoner, one whose occupation is to make arithmetical calculations," agent noun from compute (v.) Meaning "calculating machine" (of any type) is from 1897; in modern use, "programmable digital electronic device for performing mathematical or logical operations".

Here is another computer term that everyone should be familiar with:

Browser
1845, "animal which browses," agent noun from browse (v.) From 1863 as "person who browses" among books. In the *computer* sense by 1982.

Did you notice that both definitions refer to a person and not a machine? We as people are the original network and we have been "linking" and "connecting" with each other since the beginning of time.

Here's a consolidated list of the principles of networking related to both interpersonal networking and computer web connectivity. Pay attention to the similarities between the two concepts.

Principles of Networking (Interpersonal Networking):
1. Building genuine relationships
2. Practicing reciprocity
3. Being proactive and consistent
4. Being a good listener
5. Providing value and support
6. Being open-minded and respectful
7. Seeking mutual benefits
8. Cultivating a diverse network
9. Following up and staying connected
10. Giving before receiving

NETWORKING SUCCESS

Principles of Networking (Computer Web Connectivity):
1. Scalability
2. Reliability and Redundancy
3. Security
4. Quality of Service (QoS)
5. Network Monitoring and Management
6. Interoperability
7. Bandwidth Management
8. Scalable Addressing and IP Management
9. Fault Tolerance
10. Documentation and Standardization
11. Network Segmentation
12. Load Balancing
13. Network Virtualization
14. Bandwidth Optimization
15. Network Access Control
16. Network Resilience and Disaster Recovery
17. Network Performance Optimization
18. Network Automation
19. Compliance and Regulatory Considerations
20. Continuous Learning and Adaptation
21. Network Monitoring and Analysis
22. Network Traffic Management
23. Network Resiliency
24. Network Segregation and Isolation
25. Network Documentation and Change Management
26. Network Auditing and Compliance
27. Network Performance Testing and Optimization
28. Network Capacity Planning
29. Network Incident Response
30. Continuous Improvement

Computer Networking Principles

Principles of Networking (Computer Web Connectivity):

These principles, when applied effectively, contribute to the establishment of reliable, secure, and high-performance networks, whether in interpersonal relationships or computer web connectivity. Please note that these principles encompass both the interpersonal aspects of networking with others and the principles related to computers.

1. Scalability: Networking systems should be designed to handle growth and accommodate an increasing number of devices, users, and data traffic. Scalability ensures that the network can expand without compromising performance or reliability. This principle involves implementing scalable hardware, using efficient protocols, and adopting flexible network architectures.

2. Reliability and Redundancy: Networking systems should be designed to provide reliable and uninterrupted connectivity. Redundancy involves implementing backup systems, alternate paths, and failover mechanisms to ensure network availability in case of failures or disruptions. Redundant components and backup configurations minimize downtime and enhance reliability.

3. Security: Networking systems must prioritize security to protect data, prevent unauthorized access, and safeguard against threats. This includes implementing robust authentication mechanisms, encryption protocols, firewalls, intrusion detection systems, and regular security audits. Network administrators should stay updated with the latest security practices and patches to address emerging vulnerabilities.

4. Quality of Service (QoS): QoS ensures that the network can prioritize and allocate resources effectively to meet specific requirements for different applications or services. This principle involves implementing mechanisms to prioritize real-time traffic, manage bandwidth allocation, and enforce service-level agreements (SLAs) to maintain optimal performance for critical applications.

5. Network Monitoring and Management: Effective networking requires continuous monitoring and management to identify and address performance

issues, bottlenecks, and potential security threats. Network monitoring tools and protocols enable administrators to proactively detect, analyze, and resolve network-related problems. Regular monitoring and maintenance ensure optimal performance and minimize downtime.

6. Interoperability: Networking systems should support interoperability, enabling different devices, platforms, and protocols to communicate and exchange data seamlessly. Implementing open standards and protocols promotes compatibility and ensures that devices from different vendors can interoperate effectively.

7. Bandwidth Management: Efficient bandwidth management is essential for optimizing network performance and ensuring fair resource allocation. This involves implementing traffic shaping, quality-of-service mechanisms, and bandwidth optimization techniques to prioritize critical traffic, avoid congestion, and maintain an optimal user experience.

8. Scalable Addressing and IP Management: As networks grow, it is crucial to manage IP addresses efficiently. Implementing scalable addressing schemes, such as IPv6, enables the allocation of a large number of unique addresses. IP management tools and techniques help administrators track and assign IP addresses effectively.

9. Fault Tolerance: Networking systems should be designed to tolerate and recover from failures or disruptions. This includes implementing redundancy, backup configurations, and fault-tolerant protocols. Fault-tolerant systems ensure minimal disruption and quick recovery in case of network failures.

10. Documentation and Standardization: Proper documentation and standardization of network configurations, protocols, and procedures are essential for efficient management and troubleshooting. This includes maintaining up-to-date network documentation, configuration backups, and adherence to industry best practices and standards.

11. Network Segmentation: Network segmentation involves dividing a large network into smaller, isolated segments to enhance security, manage traffic, and improve performance. By segregating the network into distinct segments, such as virtual LANs (VLANs) or subnets, administrators can control access, reduce the impact of security breaches, and optimize network resources.

12. Load Balancing: Load balancing distributes network traffic across multiple resources, such as servers or network links, to optimize performance and avoid congestion. Load balancers monitor the traffic load and dynamically distribute incoming requests, ensuring even distribution and efficient utilization of resources. This principle is crucial for handling high traffic volumes and maintaining network responsiveness.

13. Network Virtualization: Network virtualization allows the creation of virtual networks, decoupled from the physical infrastructure, to enable flexible resource allocation, improved scalability, and simplified management. Virtualization technologies, such as software-defined networking (SDN) and network virtualization overlays (NVO), provide agility, efficiency, and easier deployment of network services.

14. Bandwidth Optimization: Bandwidth optimization techniques aim to maximize the utilization of available network bandwidth while minimizing congestion and delays. This includes implementing compression, caching, and traffic optimization mechanisms to reduce data size, prioritize critical traffic, and minimize the impact of latency on network performance.

15. Network Access Control: Network access control (NAC) enforces policies to authenticate and authorize devices and users accessing the network. NAC solutions validate device security posture, verify user identities, and enforce access restrictions based on predefined policies. This principle enhances network security by preventing unauthorized access and ensuring compliance with security protocols.

16. Network Resilience and Disaster Recovery: Networking systems should be designed to withstand and recover from unexpected events, such as natural disasters or equipment failures. Implementing redundant components, backup connections, and disaster recovery plans ensures network resilience and minimizes the impact of disruptions on business continuity.

17. Network Performance Optimization: Network performance optimization focuses on enhancing network speed, responsiveness, and efficiency. This includes monitoring network performance metrics, analyzing bottlenecks, fine-tuning configurations, and optimizing network protocols to achieve optimal throughput and minimize latency.

18. Network Automation: Network automation involves leveraging software-defined networking (SDN), network orchestration, and configuration management tools to automate network provisioning, monitoring, and management tasks. Automation streamlines repetitive processes, reduces human errors, and enables faster network deployment and troubleshooting.

19. Compliance and Regulatory Considerations: Networking systems must comply with industry-specific regulations, data protection laws, and security standards. This includes implementing appropriate security controls, ensuring data privacy, and adhering to compliance requirements, such as Payment Card Industry Data Security Standard (PCI DSS) or General Data Protection Regulation (GDPR).

20. Continuous Learning and Adaptation: Networking is a dynamic field, with new technologies and threats emerging regularly. It is important to stay updated with the latest industry trends, best practices, and security vulnerabilities. Networking professionals should engage in continuous learning, attend training programs, obtain relevant certifications, and actively participate in industry forums to stay abreast of advancements and adapt their networking strategies accordingly.

21. Network Monitoring and Analysis: Continuous monitoring and analysis of network performance, traffic patterns, and security events are essential for proactive network management. Network monitoring tools and techniques help administrators identify bottlenecks, troubleshoot issues, detect anomalies, and optimize network resources.

22. Network Traffic Management: Effective traffic management ensures that network resources are allocated efficiently and prioritized based on application requirements. This involves implementing traffic shaping, traffic prioritization, and Quality of Service (QoS) mechanisms to optimize network performance, minimize latency, and provide a consistent user experience.

23. Network Resiliency: Networks should be designed to withstand and recover from various types of failures or disruptions. Redundant components, backup systems, and disaster recovery plans help ensure network resiliency, minimizing downtime and maintaining business continuity.

24. Network Segregation and Isolation: Segregating and isolating network segments based on different user groups, departments, or security requirements enhances network security and controls the flow of data. This principle helps prevent unauthorized access and limits the impact of security breaches.

25. Network Documentation and Change Management: Comprehensive documentation of network configurations, topologies, and changes is crucial for effective network management and troubleshooting. Establishing change management processes ensures that network changes are documented, tested, and implemented in a controlled manner, minimizing the risk of disruptions or misconfigurations.

26. Network Auditing and Compliance: Regular network auditing and compliance assessments help identify vulnerabilities, ensure adherence to security policies, and validate regulatory compliance. Network audits involve evaluating network configurations, access controls, and security measures to maintain a secure and compliant networking environment.

27. Network Performance Testing and Optimization: Rigorous testing of network performance under varying conditions helps identify bottlenecks, assess scalability, and optimize network configurations. Performance testing tools and techniques simulate real-world scenarios to ensure that the network meets the required performance benchmarks.

28. Network Capacity Planning: Capacity planning involves predicting future network requirements and ensuring that sufficient resources are available to support the anticipated growth in traffic, users, and applications. Proper capacity planning avoids performance degradation, optimizes resource allocation, and allows for seamless network expansion.

29. Network Incident Response: Establishing an incident response plan ensures a swift and effective response to network security incidents, breaches, or disruptions. This includes defining roles and responsibilities, establishing incident response procedures, and conducting post-incident analysis to prevent similar incidents in the future.

30. Continuous Improvement: Networking is an ongoing process, and continuous improvement is crucial for adapting to changing technologies, addressing emerging threats, and optimizing network performance. Regular evaluation, feedback loops, and a culture of continuous improvement help identify areas for enhancement and drive innovation in networking practices.

I hope that you all have noticed that computers are based off the human model of networking. The same principles of security, ability to scale, continuous improvement in relations, overcoming failures, and the like are not just computer terms but have their beginning in our human experience. We can look to the computer to give us an idea of how we network in the physical world. The principles of human relations were applied to the computer. I want you to exercise caution that you do not treat your relationships like a machine. A machine is only as good as its programmer. A machine can never be better then you because humans do not all operate by the same "instructions". Our DNA, while sharing some similarities, is varied greatly among the global populations and carries numerable combinations that make every person a unique individual.

Follow me to the next section to discover some quantitative information about networking.

The Proof that Networking Works

Here are some insights and observations regarding the impact of networking. It's important to note that the effectiveness of networking can vary depending on factors such as industry, individual efforts, and the specific goals of networking. Here are some key points to consider:

1. **The Power of Referrals**: Referrals are often cited as one of the most effective methods of generating business or finding job opportunities. According to a study by LinkedIn, approximately 85% of jobs are filled through networking and referrals. Personal recommendations and introductions from trusted connections can significantly increase your chances of success.

2. **Relationship Building**: Networking is primarily about building relationships and fostering connections. According to a survey conducted by HubSpot, 95% of professionals said that face-to-face meetings are essential for building long-term business relationships. Building a strong network of contacts can provide support, opportunities, and valuable insights.

3. **Business Growth**: Effective networking can contribute to business growth and lead generation. The Harvard Business Review reported that 84% of business executives believe that networking plays a significant role in their business success. Networking allows entrepreneurs and business professionals to expand their reach, discover new clients or customers, and explore potential partnerships or collaborations.

4. **Career Advancement**: Networking is crucial for career development and advancement. According to a survey by the Adler Group, 85% of all jobs are filled through networking. Making connections with professionals in your field can lead to job opportunities, career mentorship, and access to insider information. It can also provide exposure to new ideas and industry trends.

5. **Access to Resources and Knowledge**: Effective networking provides access to valuable resources, knowledge, and expertise. Engaging with a diverse network allows you to tap into the collective wisdom of professionals who have different perspectives and experiences. You can gain insights, advice, and guidance from industry experts, which can be instrumental in your personal and professional growth.

On the other hand, networking can be ineffective if not approached strategically or if certain challenges arise:

1. **Lack of Focus**: Networking without clear goals or objectives can be ineffective. It's essential to identify the specific outcomes you want to achieve through networking, whether it's finding job opportunities, expanding your client base, or gaining industry insights. Without focus, networking efforts may lack direction and result in scattered connections without meaningful outcomes.

2. **Inauthentic Interactions**: Networking can be ineffective if approached with a purely transactional mindset. If individuals come across as disingenuous or solely interested in what they can gain, it can hinder the development of authentic connections. Networking should be about building mutually beneficial relationships, offering support, and adding value to others.

3. **Lack of Follow-up**: Building a network is not just about initial interactions; it requires consistent nurturing and follow-up. Failure to follow up with contacts or maintain regular communication can limit the effectiveness of networking efforts. Without sustained engagement, connections may fade over time, and opportunities may be missed.

4. **Networking Burnout**: Networking requires time and energy. Engaging in too many networking events or activities without proper balance and self-care can lead to burnout. It's important to be selective in choosing networking opportunities and prioritize quality over quantity.

After looking at the numbers and track record of networking, we can see how having a strategy can be very beneficial to avoid the negative effects of improper networking. You must begin your plan of attack from within. You must have awareness and knowledge of yourself to deal with other people effectively. Let us look at a bodily system that is connected to the various with which we network.

Networking and Your Body

The solar plexus, also known as the celiac plexus, is a complex network of nerves located in the upper abdomen, behind the stomach. It plays a crucial role in the functioning of various organs and systems in the body. While the direct correlation of the solar plexus to networking may be symbolic rather than physiological, we can explore the interconnected parts of the solar plexus and their functions to draw insights for successful networking with others. Here are the key components and their potential correlations:

1. Nerves: The solar plexus consists of a network of nerves that branch out to various organs, including the stomach, liver, gallbladder, pancreas, and intestines. These nerves facilitate communication and coordination between these organs, ensuring their proper functioning. In the context of networking, nerves can symbolize effective communication and connection-building skills. Successful networking relies on clear and effective communication to establish and maintain meaningful relationships.

2. Stomach: The solar plexus is closely connected to the stomach, which is responsible for digestion and nourishment. In networking, the stomach can represent the exchange of ideas, knowledge, and resources. Just as the stomach processes and absorbs nutrients, successful networking involves sharing and exchanging valuable insights, expertise, and support with others.

3. Liver and Gallbladder: The liver and gallbladder play important roles in metabolism, detoxification, and storage of essential substances. In the context of

networking, these organs can represent the ability to adapt and respond effectively to different situations. Successful networking often requires flexibility, adaptability, and the capacity to navigate diverse environments and personalities.

4. Pancreas: The pancreas plays a vital role in regulating blood sugar levels and producing digestive enzymes. It ensures a balanced internal environment. In the realm of networking, the pancreas can symbolize emotional intelligence and empathy. Understanding and regulating emotions, as well as perceiving the emotional states of others, are essential for establishing authentic connections and fostering meaningful relationships.

5. Intestines: The intestines are responsible for the digestion and absorption of nutrients, as well as the elimination of waste. In the context of networking, the intestines can represent the ability to filter and process information effectively. Successful networking requires discernment and the capacity to absorb valuable insights while filtering out unnecessary or irrelevant information.

6. Nervous System: The solar plexus is a key hub of the autonomic nervous system, which controls various bodily functions. Networking requires engaging with others, building rapport, and establishing connections. Just as the nerves in the solar plexus facilitate communication between organs, the ability to effectively communicate and connect with others is essential for successful networking. Networking involves active listening, clear articulation of ideas, and the ability to convey thoughts and emotions in a relatable manner.

7. Confidence and Assertiveness: The solar plexus is often associated with personal power and self-confidence. Successful networking requires a level of confidence and assertiveness to approach new people, initiate conversations, and present oneself with authenticity. A strong solar plexus can be symbolic of the inner strength and self-assuredness needed to navigate networking opportunities with grace and confidence.

8. Gut Instinct and Intuition: The solar plexus is sometimes referred to as the "gut brain" due to its connection with instinctual feelings and intuition. Networking involves making choices about whom to connect with, whom to trust, and which opportunities to pursue. Developing and trusting your intuition can guide you in making wise decisions and forming meaningful connections in your network.

9. Emotional Resilience: The solar plexus is closely tied to emotional well-being. Successful networking often involves facing rejection, overcoming obstacles, and

handling various emotions that arise during interactions. Developing emotional resilience and maintaining a balanced emotional state can help you navigate the ups and downs of networking with grace and perseverance.

10. Energy Exchange: The solar plexus is associated with the concept of energy exchange in various spiritual practices. Networking involves giving and receiving energy, support, and resources. Being mindful of the energy you bring to networking interactions and ensuring a mutually beneficial exchange can contribute to building and sustaining strong relationships within your network.

11. Alignment with Purpose: The solar plexus is connected to personal identity and purpose. Successful networking is often driven by a sense of purpose and shared values. When networking aligns with your core beliefs and passions, it becomes more meaningful and authentic. Clarifying your purpose and aligning it with your networking efforts can attract like-minded individuals and lead to deeper connections.

12. Trust and Vulnerability: The solar plexus is associated with feelings of trust and vulnerability. Networking requires building trust with others and being open to vulnerability, as it fosters authentic connections. Trusting your instincts, being genuine, and allowing yourself to be vulnerable can deepen the bonds within your network and lead to more meaningful relationships.

13. Resilience and Adaptability: The solar plexus is linked to the body's ability to adapt and recover from stress. Networking often involves encountering diverse personalities, navigating challenging situations, and adapting to different environments. Developing resilience and adaptability helps you stay composed and flexible, enabling you to overcome obstacles and build connections even in unfamiliar or demanding circumstances.

14. Collaboration and Synergy: The solar plexus represents the interconnectedness of organs within the body. Similarly, successful networking often involves collaboration and synergistic relationships. By recognizing the strengths and expertise of others and fostering a spirit of collaboration, you can create synergies within your network that lead to mutual growth and success.

15. Personal Growth and Expansion: The solar plexus is associated with personal growth and expansion. Networking provides opportunities for learning, exposure to new ideas, and expanding your horizons. By actively seeking out diverse

perspectives and experiences, you can fuel your personal growth and expand your network, ultimately contributing to your overall success.

16. Gratitude and Abundance: The solar plexus is associated with a sense of gratitude and abundance. Networking from a mindset of gratitude allows you to appreciate the connections and opportunities that come your way. Recognizing and expressing gratitude for the people in your network and the support you receive cultivates a positive atmosphere, reinforcing the abundance of resources and opportunities available through networking.

17. Authenticity and Integrity: The solar plexus represents personal power and authenticity. Successful networking requires authenticity and integrity in your interactions. Being true to yourself, expressing your values, and acting with integrity.

18. Continuous Learning and Improvement: The solar plexus is connected to the body's continuous growth and improvement. Networking involves ongoing learning, refining your communication skills, and staying updated on industry trends. Embracing a growth mindset and being open to learning and improvement will help you adapt to changing networking dynamics and stay relevant in your field.

19. Empathy and Understanding: The solar plexus is connected to emotional intelligence and empathy. Successful networking involves understanding the needs, perspectives, and emotions of others. Developing empathy allows you to connect with people on a deeper level, fostering stronger relationships and facilitating effective collaboration.

20. Boundaries and Self-Care: The solar plexus is associated with establishing boundaries and maintaining balance. Networking requires setting boundaries to protect your time, energy, and well-being. Prioritizing self-care ensures that you have the capacity to engage with others authentically and sustainably, avoiding burnout and maintaining a healthy work-life balance.

21. Intention and Focus: The solar plexus represents personal intention and focus. Successful networking requires clarity of purpose and a focused approach. Setting clear intentions for your networking efforts helps you prioritize opportunities that align with your goals and values, enabling you to make meaningful connections and achieve desired outcomes.

22. Resonance and Connection: The solar plexus is associated with resonance and energetic alignment. In networking, the concept of resonance refers to connecting with individuals who share similar values, interests, or goals. Building connections based on resonance creates a natural affinity, enhancing the quality and authenticity of your network relationships.

23. Influence and Leadership: The solar plexus represents personal power and influence. Successful networking often involves demonstrating leadership qualities and influencing others positively. By showcasing your expertise, providing value to others, and leading by example, you can establish yourself as a trusted and respected individual within your network.

24. Graciousness and Appreciation: The solar plexus is connected to feelings of gratitude and appreciation. Successful networking involves acknowledging and expressing gratitude for the support, guidance, and opportunities received from others. Cultivating graciousness and showing appreciation for the contributions of individuals in your network strengthens the bonds and fosters a supportive environment.

25. Serendipity and Synchronicity: The solar plexus represents the interconnectedness of events and experiences. Networking often brings unexpected encounters, opportunities, and collaborations. Embracing serendipity and being open to synchronistic connections allows you to make the most of these fortuitous moments, leading to valuable connections and unexpected growth.

Remember, these correlations draw upon the symbolism and metaphorical associations of the solar plexus. They provide insights and perspectives that can be applied to enhance your networking experiences. By embodying these qualities and principles, you can cultivate a mindset and approach that supports successful networking, fosters meaningful connections, and contributes to your personal and professional development.

Developing effective communication, self-confidence, intuition, emotional resilience, and aligning with purpose can contribute to building a strong network and forging meaningful relationships with others. By nurturing these qualities within yourself, you can enhance your networking abilities and create valuable connections that support your personal and professional growth.

The interconnected parts of the solar plexus and networking can provide insights into the qualities and skills that contribute to successful networking. Effective communication, the exchange of valuable resources and ideas, adaptability, emotional intelligence, and discernment are all important aspects of building and nurturing a strong network of relationships. By recognizing and developing these qualities within us, we can enhance our networking abilities and foster meaningful connections with others.

Next up for discussion is the efficiencies and deficiencies of networking.

Efficiencies and deficiencies of networking

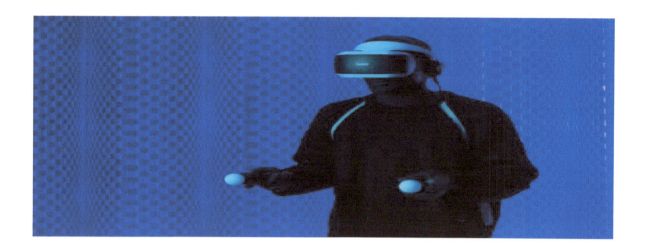

1. Networking Effectiveness:

Increased Opportunities:
Effective networking expands your professional opportunities. According to a study by the American Sociological Review, individuals with larger and more diverse networks have greater access to information, resources, and job opportunities.

Knowledge Sharing:
Networking allows for the exchange of knowledge and expertise. By connecting with professionals in different fields or industries, you can gain insights, learn from their experiences, and stay updated on industry trends. This knowledge can enhance your decision-making and problem-solving abilities.

Enhanced Professional Reputation:
Building a strong network can contribute to your professional reputation. When you consistently engage with others in a positive and meaningful way, you establish yourself as a reliable and trustworthy individual. Your reputation can lead to referrals, recommendations, and increased credibility.

Personal Development:
Effective networking provides opportunities for personal growth and development. Engaging with individuals from diverse backgrounds exposes you to new perspectives, challenges your assumptions, and broadens your horizons. This exposure can foster personal growth and help you develop valuable skills such as communication, negotiation, and relationship-building.

Collaborative Opportunities:
Effective networking can lead to collaborative opportunities. By connecting with professionals who share similar goals or complementary skills, you can explore collaborations, joint projects, or partnerships. Collaborative efforts can enhance your capabilities, expand your reach, and open doors to new opportunities.

Personal Support:
Networking provides a support system of like-minded individuals who can offer guidance, advice, and mentorship. Building relationships with experienced professionals in your field can provide invaluable support and help you navigate challenges or transitions in your career.

Industry Insights:
Networking allows you to gain valuable industry insights and stay informed about market trends, technological advancements, and best practices. Engaging with professionals who have diverse perspectives and experiences can broaden your understanding and help you stay ahead in your field.

Access to Hidden Opportunities:
Networking often provides access to hidden job opportunities or projects that may not be advertised publicly. Through your connections, you may learn about job openings, consulting opportunities, or upcoming projects that are not yet widely known. This gives you a competitive advantage in pursuing these opportunities.

Social Capital:
Effective networking helps you build social capital, which refers to the value derived from your relationships, connections, and networks. Social capital provides access to resources, information, and opportunities that can positively impact your personal and professional life. It enables you to leverage the collective knowledge and influence of your network for mutual benefits.

Professional Development:
Networking offers opportunities for professional development. Engaging with industry leaders, attending conferences or workshops, and participating in networking events can broaden your knowledge, sharpen your skills, and expose you to new ideas and perspectives. By staying connected with professionals who are ahead in their fields, you can learn from their experiences and stay updated on industry trends.

Emotional Support:
Effective networking provides emotional support and a sense of belonging. Having a network of trusted professionals who understand your challenges and can offer support, encouragement, and empathy can be invaluable. Networking can help alleviate feelings of isolation and provide a platform for sharing experiences and seeking advice.

Personal Branding:
Networking allows you to build and promote your personal brand. By consistently engaging with others, sharing your expertise, and showcasing your unique value proposition, you can establish yourself as an authority or thought leader in your field. This enhances your visibility, credibility, and professional reputation.

2. Networking Ineffectiveness:

Lack of Strategy:
Networking without a clear strategy or purpose can be ineffective. Attending events or joining groups randomly without a focused approach may lead to scattered connections without tangible outcomes. It's important to identify your goals, target specific industries or communities, and prioritize events or activities that align with your objectives.

Superficial Interactions:
Networking can be ineffective if interactions remain surface-level and lack depth. Engaging in meaningful conversations and actively listening to others' perspectives builds stronger connections. Superficial interactions often fail to establish a genuine rapport and may not lead to meaningful relationships or opportunities.

Neglecting Relationship Maintenance:
Building a network requires ongoing effort. Neglecting to nurture relationships or failing to follow up can lead to missed opportunities. It's crucial to stay in touch with your contacts, provide support when needed, and contribute value to the relationship over time

Overemphasis on Immediate Gains:
Networking should be a long-term investment rather than solely focusing on immediate gains. Building genuine relationships takes time, and expecting immediate returns may hinder your networking effectiveness. Patience, consistency, and a willingness to provide value without expecting immediate reciprocity are important for long-term success.

Inadequate Preparation:
Networking events or meetings require preparation to make the most of the opportunities presented. Lack of preparation can result in missed connections or ineffective interactions. Research the event or individuals attending, prepare meaningful conversation starters, and have your elevator pitch ready to make a strong impression.

Lack of Follow-through:
Simply exchanging business cards or making initial connections is not enough. Networking becomes ineffective when there is a lack of follow-through. Failing to follow up, maintain regular communication, or deliver on commitments can lead to missed opportunities and a loss of credibility.

Lack of Authenticity:
Authenticity is crucial in networking. Ineffective networking occurs when individuals present a false image or try to impress others without being genuine. Building relationships based on trust and authenticity is essential for long-term success in networking.

Overlooking Diversity:
Networking becomes ineffective when there is a lack of diversity in your connections. Expanding your network to include individuals from different backgrounds, cultures, and industries can bring fresh perspectives and new

opportunities. Embracing diversity in your network enhances creativity, innovation, and problem-solving abilities.

Excessive Self-Promotion:
Networking is about building mutually beneficial relationships, not just self-promotion. Individuals who focus solely on promoting themselves without showing interest in others' needs or contributions may be perceived as self-centered. Effective networking involves a balance of sharing and listening, demonstrating a genuine interest in others.

Failure to Adapt:
Networking is an ever-evolving process, and ineffective networking occurs when individuals fail to adapt to changing circumstances or emerging trends. Being flexible, open-minded, and receptive to new ideas and technologies is essential to maintain an effective network.

Lack of Proactive Approach:
Ineffective networking often results from a passive approach where individuals wait for opportunities to come to them instead of actively seeking them out. Networking requires proactivity, initiative, and a willingness to put yourself out there. Taking the initiative to reach out, attend events, and follow up on connections is crucial for networking success.

Overlooking Relationship Building:
Networking is not just about collecting business cards or expanding your contact list. It's about building meaningful relationships based on trust, mutual respect, and shared interests. Ineffective networking occurs when individuals focus solely on transactional interactions without investing time and effort in cultivating genuine connections.

Failure to Give and Receive:
Networking is a two-way street. It's important to approach networking with a mindset of giving and receiving. Ineffective networking occurs when individuals are only focused on what they can gain without offering support or adding value to others. Building strong relationships requires a willingness to give assistance, share insights, and offer help when needed.

Lack of Active Listening:
Effective networking involves active listening and genuine interest in others. Ineffective networking occurs when individuals dominate conversations, fail to listen attentively, or show disinterest in what others have to say. Active listening allows you to understand others' needs, identify potential synergies, and forge stronger connections.

Inconsistency and Inertia:
Networking requires consistent effort and engagement. Ineffective networking occurs when individuals are inconsistent in their networking activities or become complacent after making initial connections. Building and maintaining a network requires ongoing nurturing, follow-up, and active participation in relevant events and communities.

By considering these factors and avoiding common pitfalls, you can enhance the effectiveness of your networking efforts. Networking is a skill that can be developed and refined with practice, persistence, and a genuine desire to build meaningful connections.

Remember that networking is a continuous process that requires ongoing effort, genuine engagement, and a willingness to give and receive support. With dedication and the right approach, you can build a strong and valuable network that enriches your personal and professional life. With time and deliberate practice, you can refine your networking skills and create a valuable network that supports your personal and professional aspirations.

While specific statistics on networking effectiveness and ineffectiveness may be limited, these insights highlight the potential impact and benefits of effective networking. By approaching networking strategically, building genuine relationships, and staying focused on your goals, you can maximize the effectiveness of your networking efforts.

The Reason Most People Fail at Networking

Incorrect networking, or difficulties in establishing effective connections and relationships with others, can have various causes. Here are some potential factors that can contribute to problems in networking:

1. Lack of Social Skills: Some individuals may struggle with social skills such as communication, active listening, empathy, or understanding non-verbal cues. These deficiencies can make it challenging for them to initiate and maintain meaningful connections with others.

2. Shyness or Social Anxiety: People who are naturally introverted or experience social anxiety may find it difficult to approach and interact with new individuals. Feelings of discomfort, self-consciousness, or fear of rejection can hinder their networking abilities.

3. Limited Networking Opportunities: In certain circumstances, individuals may have limited exposure to networking opportunities. For example, someone in a small town or a niche industry may find it challenging to meet new people or expand their professional network.

4. Lack of Confidence: Low self-confidence can undermine networking efforts. When individuals doubt their abilities or fear judgment, they may hesitate to reach out to others or share their ideas, making it harder to establish connections.

5. Communication Barriers: Effective networking often requires clear and concise communication. Language barriers, cultural differences, or unfamiliarity with communication norms can impede effective networking, particularly in multicultural or international settings.

6. Unfavorable Attitudes: Negative attitudes, such as arrogance, insensitivity, or a lack of interest in others, can hinder networking efforts. People tend to be more receptive to those who demonstrate genuine interest, positivity, and respect.

7. Ineffective Networking Strategies: Some individuals may lack knowledge of effective networking strategies, such as identifying shared interests, leveraging existing connections, or maintaining a proactive online presence. Without a strategic approach, networking attempts may be less successful.

8. Mismatched Expectations: Misalignment in expectations can lead to networking challenges. For instance, if one person seeks a mutually beneficial professional connection, while the other expects immediate favors or benefits, the relationship may not develop harmoniously.

9. Past Negative Experiences: Negative experiences in previous networking attempts, such as rejection, betrayal, or disappointment, can create psychological barriers that hinder future networking efforts. Individuals may become guarded or hesitant to engage with others due to fear of repeating negative experiences.

10. Lack of Follow-up: Networking requires consistent effort and follow-up. Failing to maintain connections, respond promptly to inquiries, or nurture relationships can result in missed opportunities and weakened networking effectiveness.

11. Lack of Authenticity: Networking is most successful when individuals can genuinely express themselves and connect with others on a deeper level. If someone adopts a false persona or tries to impress others by being someone they're not, it can hinder the development of genuine connections and trust.

12. Overreliance on Technology: While technology and social media platforms provide valuable networking opportunities, excessive reliance on virtual

interactions can lead to a lack of face-to-face networking skills. Over-reliance on online communication may result in difficulties establishing meaningful connections in person.

13. Inadequate Preparation: Networking events or meetings require preparation to make a positive impression. Lack of preparation, including not researching the individuals or organizations one wishes to connect with, can lead to missed opportunities or ineffective networking attempts.

14. Inability to Handle Rejection: Rejection is a common aspect of networking. Some individuals may struggle to handle rejection or take it personally, which can lead to discouragement or reluctance to continue networking efforts.

15. Lack of Networking Strategy: Networking without a clear strategy or goal can make the process less effective. It's important to identify the purpose behind networking (e.g., job search, business opportunities, professional growth) and develop a plan to achieve specific objectives.

16. Limited Diverse Connections: Networking within a small or homogeneous circle can restrict exposure to different perspectives, opportunities, and resources. Lack of diverse connections may hinder personal and professional growth and limit the breadth of networking opportunities.

17. Lack of Reciprocity: Networking is built on the principle of mutual benefit. Failing to contribute, support, or offer assistance to others can lead to a one-sided network where individuals are less inclined to reciprocate or engage in meaningful exchanges.

18. External Factors: Various external factors, such as time constraints, work overload, personal circumstances, or environmental factors, can impact networking efforts. These factors may limit the time and energy individuals can invest in networking, affecting their ability to establish and nurture connections effectively.

19. Cultural or Social Norms: Different cultures and social contexts have distinct networking norms. Failing to understand or adapt to these norms, such as appropriate behavior, communication styles, or social etiquette, can hinder networking efforts in specific cultural or social settings.

20. Lack of Persistence: Building a strong network takes time and persistence. Some individuals may give up too easily after encountering initial obstacles or

setbacks, missing out on potential opportunities that may arise with continued effort.

21. Lack of Emotional Intelligence: Emotional intelligence involves the ability to recognize and understand one's own emotions and those of others. Individuals with low emotional intelligence may struggle to navigate social dynamics, empathize with others, or adapt their behavior to different situations, which can hinder effective networking.

22. Unfocused Approach: Networking without a clear focus or target audience can lead to scattered efforts and limited results. It is important to identify specific industries, communities, or professional circles that align with one's goals and invest energy in building connections within those areas.

23. Inability to Leverage Weak Ties: Weak ties refer to acquaintances or connections that are not close friends or family. Research has shown that weak ties often provide valuable networking opportunities and access to new information and resources. Individuals who fail to recognize the potential of weak ties may miss out on networking benefits.

24. Lack of Personal Branding: Personal branding involves cultivating a positive and consistent image that represents one's skills, values, and expertise. Without a clear personal brand, individuals may struggle to stand out and differentiate themselves in networking situations, making it harder to build meaningful connections.

25. Inability to Navigate Power Dynamics: Networking often involves navigating power dynamics, such as interacting with individuals in positions of authority or seniority. Some individuals may feel intimidated or struggle to assert themselves in such situations, impacting their ability to network effectively.

26. Lack of Boundaries: Networking requires establishing and maintaining healthy boundaries. Failing to set boundaries can result in overcommitment, burnout, or being taken advantage of, ultimately hindering networking efforts.

27. Limited Networking Resources: Access to networking resources, such as industry events, professional associations, or mentorship programs, can significantly impact networking opportunities. Individuals in disadvantaged or underrepresented groups may face additional barriers in accessing these resources, affecting their networking effectiveness.

28. Negative Self-Talk or Limiting Beliefs: Negative self-talk and limiting beliefs can undermine one's confidence and hinder networking efforts. Thoughts such as "I'm not good enough" or "I don't have anything valuable to offer" can prevent individuals from putting themselves out there and engaging in effective networking.

29. Fear of Networking Stereotypes: Networking stereotypes, such as the perception that it's solely driven by self-interest or that it involves superficial interactions, can deter individuals from engaging in networking. Overcoming these stereotypes and recognizing the potential for genuine connections is crucial for effective networking.

30. Lack of Persistence in Relationship Building: Building strong connections requires ongoing effort and nurturing. Some individuals may struggle with maintaining long-term relationships, leading to a lack of depth in their network and missed opportunities for collaboration or support.

31. Inauthentic Networking Events: Attending networking events that are poorly organized, lack a genuine networking atmosphere, or focus solely on sales pitches can hinder meaningful connections. It is important to choose events that align with one's goals and values, where authentic networking opportunities are more likely to arise.

32. Lack of Active Networking: Networking is an active process that requires proactive engagement. Merely attending events or having a large number of connections on social media is not sufficient. Taking the initiative to reach out, follow up, and maintain regular communication is crucial for effective networking.

33. Overlooking Niche Networks: In addition to general networking opportunities, niche networks or specialized communities related to specific industries, interests, or demographics can provide unique networking advantages. Overlooking these networks may limit the potential for targeted connections and opportunities.

34. Inadequate Networking Tools: Utilizing appropriate networking tools, both online and offline, can enhance networking effectiveness. These tools can include professional networking platforms, business cards, online portfolios, or personal websites that showcase skills, experience, and interests.

35. Lack of Diverse Perspectives: Surrounding oneself with individuals who share similar backgrounds, experiences, or perspectives can limit networking outcomes. Engaging with people from diverse backgrounds and perspectives fosters innovation, creativity, and a broader range of opportunities.

36. Failure to Follow Ethical Networking Practices: Unethical networking practices, such as using connections solely for personal gain without reciprocation, spreading false information, or misrepresenting oneself, can damage professional reputation and hinder networking success. Adhering to ethical principles builds trust and fosters strong connections.

37. Lack of Networking Mentorship or Guidance: Networking skills can be developed and refined through mentorship or guidance from experienced networkers. Seeking out mentors or coaches who can provide insights, advice, and support in navigating networking challenges can be highly beneficial.

38. Overlooking the Power of Referrals: Networking is not solely about direct connections; it also involves leveraging referrals. Building strong relationships with existing connections who can vouch for one's skills, expertise, or character can lead to valuable introductions and increased networking opportunities.

39. Failure to Adapt to Changing Networking Trends: Networking practices and platforms evolve over time. Staying updated on emerging trends, such as utilizing social media platforms, virtual networking events, or online communities, allows individuals to adapt and maximize networking opportunities in the digital age.

40. Ignoring Personal Development: Personal growth and self-improvement contribute significantly to networking effectiveness. Investing in developing skills, expanding knowledge, and fostering a positive mindset enhances confidence, conversation skills, and the ability to add value to networking interactions.

41. Lack of Follow-Through: Networking efforts may fall short if individuals fail to follow through on commitments or promises made during networking interactions. It is important to deliver on agreed-upon actions, provide requested information, or follow up with contacts in a timely manner to maintain credibility and build trust.

42. Overwhelming Focus on Quantity over Quality: While expanding one's network is important, solely prioritizing quantity over quality can lead to superficial connections. Focusing on building deeper, meaningful relationships

with a select group of individuals who align with one's goals and values can yield more fruitful networking outcomes.

43. Overlooking Non-Traditional Networking Opportunities: Networking opportunities can arise in unexpected places, beyond formal networking events or professional settings. Community involvement, volunteering, hobby groups, or even casual social gatherings can provide avenues for networking and forming connections.

44. Lack of Active Listening: Active listening is a critical skill in networking. Individuals who dominate conversations, fail to show genuine interest in others, or are distracted by external factors may miss valuable insights and opportunities for connection. Practicing active listening promotes better understanding and fosters stronger relationships.

45. Failure to Adapt Networking Style: Effective networking requires adaptability to different situations, cultures, and communication styles. Individuals who rigidly adhere to a single networking approach may struggle to connect with individuals who have diverse backgrounds and preferences, limiting their networking potential.

46. Lack of Persistence in Relationship Maintenance: Building a network is not a one-time event but an ongoing process. Failing to nurture and maintain relationships over time can result in missed opportunities and a weakening of the network. Regular check-ins, sharing relevant information, and offering support are essential for maintaining strong connections.

47. Failure to Engage in Reciprocal Networking: Networking is a two-way street. Individuals who solely focus on their own needs or interests without offering support or assistance to others may find it challenging to establish mutually beneficial relationships. Engaging in reciprocal networking, where both parties benefit, strengthens connections and fosters long-term collaborations.

48. Reluctance to Seek Help or Ask for Support: Networking is not a solo endeavor, and individuals may encounter obstacles or challenges along the way. Reluctance to seek guidance, advice, or support from mentors, peers, or established network connections can hinder networking progress. Being open to seeking help enhances learning and growth.

49. Failure to Adapt to Cultural Nuances: Networking practices can vary across cultures, and it is essential to be aware of and adapt to cultural nuances when networking internationally or within diverse communities. Understanding cultural norms, etiquette, and communication styles promotes effective cross-cultural connections.

50. Lack of Persistence in Building Rapport: Building rapport is a crucial aspect of networking. Individuals who rush through conversations, fail to invest time in getting to know others, or lack genuine interest may struggle to establish connections. Taking the time to build rapport fosters trust and strengthens networking relationships.

Overcoming the Fears

Networking can sometimes be intimidating, with fears such as rejection, self-promotion, or social anxiety hindering effective networking. Here are list of some common fears when it comes to networking that include how to overcome these challenges:

1. Challenge Fear of Rejection: Remember that rejection is a natural part of networking. Focus on the potential opportunities and positive outcomes that can arise from successful connections.

2. Embrace Active Listening: Instead of solely focusing on self-promotion, practice active listening. Show genuine interest in others' stories and experiences, which fosters deeper connections and meaningful conversations.

3. Develop Confidence: Build confidence by celebrating small networking wins, recognizing your accomplishments, and reframing negative thoughts with positive affirmations.

4. Seek Support and Guidance: Reach out to mentors, coaches, or trusted friends for support and guidance. They can provide valuable insights, advice, and encouragement during the networking process.

Several fears can hinder people from networking effectively. Here are some additional common fears and detailed strategies to overcome them:

1. Fear of Rejection: The fear of being rejected or ignored can prevent individuals from reaching out and initiating networking conversations.

To overcome this fear:

  - Remember that rejection is a natural part of networking. Not everyone you approach will be available or interested, and that's okay. Don't take it personally.
  - Focus on the potential positive outcomes of networking, such as building valuable connections, gaining insights, or discovering new opportunities. Keep your goals in mind to motivate yourself.
  - Start small and gradually build your confidence. Begin by reaching out to acquaintances or attending smaller networking events to practice your networking skills.

2. Fear of Feeling Inauthentic: Some people worry that networking might require them to be inauthentic or fake.

To overcome this fear:

   - Embrace your authentic self. Networking is about building genuine connections, so be true to who you are. Focus on finding common ground and shared interests with others rather than trying to impress or conform to expectations.
   - Develop a mindset of giving and adding value to others. When you approach networking with the intention of helping and supporting others, it becomes more authentic and meaningful.
   - Be a good listener. Show genuine interest in others and ask thoughtful questions. This allows you to engage in meaningful conversations and build connections based on mutual understanding.

3. Fear of Networking Events or Crowded Spaces: Some individuals feel anxious or overwhelmed in large networking events or crowded spaces.

To overcome this fear:

   - Prepare in advance. Research the event, its attendees, and potential topics of conversation. Having some talking points or questions in mind can help alleviate anxiety.
   - Arrive early or contact organizers beforehand to get a lay of the land and feel more comfortable in the environment.
   - Start conversations with smaller groups or approach individuals who appear approachable and open. Remember, many people at networking events are also looking to connect, so you're not alone in seeking new connections.

4. Fear of Self-Promotion: Many people feel uncomfortable promoting themselves or their accomplishments.

To overcome this fear:

   - Shift your mindset from self-promotion to building relationships. Networking is about fostering connections and mutually beneficial interactions. Focus on understanding others' needs and how you can support them rather than solely promoting yourself.

- Practice sharing your experiences and achievements in a humble and authentic manner. Frame your accomplishments as learning opportunities or contributions to a team or project.
- Prepare an elevator pitch that concisely describes who you are, what you do, and what you're passionate about. Having this prepared can help you feel more confident when introducing yourself.

5. Fear of Not Knowing What to Say: Some individuals fear not knowing what to say or how to keep a conversation flowing.

To overcome this fear:

- Prepare a few conversation starters or open-ended questions that can initiate discussions. This can include asking about someone's professional background, current projects, or industry trends.
- Active listening is key. Pay attention to what the other person is saying, ask follow-up questions, and show genuine interest in their responses. This keeps the conversation engaging and demonstrates your attentiveness.
- Practice active observation and look for common interests or experiences that can spark conversations. It could be a shared hobby, a recent news article, or a professional challenge you both have encountered.

6. Fear of Feeling Like a Burden:

Some individuals worry that networking may make them come across as burdensome or bothersome to others. To overcome this fear:

- Remember that networking is a two-way street. Approach conversations with the mindset of mutual benefit and look for opportunities to offer support or value to others.
- Be respectful of others' time and boundaries. Approach networking conversations with a considerate and polite demeanor and be mindful of cues indicating if someone is not available for an extended conversation.
- Offer assistance or resources when appropriate. Actively listen to the needs or challenges others express and see if you can provide guidance, connections, or insights.

7. Fear of Feeling Like an Imposter: Many individuals fear that they will be perceived as an imposter or that they don't belong in certain networking circles. To overcome this fear:

   - Recognize that feeling like an imposter is a common experience that many people face. Remember your accomplishments and the value you bring to the table.
   - Shift your focus from self-doubt to curiosity and learning. Approach networking as an opportunity to expand your knowledge, gain insights from others, and grow both personally and professionally.
   - Remember that everyone has unique experiences and perspectives to offer. Embrace the diversity of ideas and expertise that can be found in networking interactions.

8. Fear of Networking Online: With the rise of virtual networking, some individuals may feel uncomfortable or unsure about how to effectively network online.

To overcome this fear:

   - Familiarize yourself with online networking platforms and tools. Explore features such as virtual events, discussion forums, or video conferences. Take the time to learn how to navigate and utilize these platforms effectively.
   - Prepare a professional online presence. Update your social media profiles, ensure your LinkedIn profile is complete, and consider creating a personal website or portfolio to showcase your skills and experiences.
   - Engage actively in online discussions and groups. Share valuable insights, ask questions, and contribute to conversations. This demonstrates your expertise and helps you build connections with like-minded individuals.

9. Fear of Follow-Up: After initial networking interactions, some individuals may feel anxious about following up with new connections.

To overcome this fear:

   - Be proactive in following up. Send a brief, personalized message to express your gratitude for the conversation and reiterate your interest in staying connected.
   - Provide value in your follow-up. Share relevant resources, articles, or insights that align with the interests or challenges discussed during the networking interaction.

- Find common ground for continued engagement. Look for opportunities to collaborate, attend future events together, or connect on shared interests.

10. Fear of Networking with Higher-Ranking Professionals: Networking with individuals in higher positions or more experienced professionals can be intimidating for some.

To overcome this fear:

- Remember that networking is about building relationships, not solely about status or hierarchy. Approach these interactions with a mindset of mutual learning and support.
- Prepare thoughtful questions or topics of discussion that demonstrate your interest in their expertise or experiences. This shows your genuine curiosity and can help level the playing field in the conversation.
- Don't underestimate your value and perspective. Recognize that you have unique insights to offer, even if you're early in your career or less experienced.

11. Fear of Networking as an Introvert: Introverted individuals may fear the social energy required for networking activities.

To overcome this fear:

- Play to your strengths as an introvert. Focus on deepening one-on-one conversations rather than trying to engage in large group settings.
- Take breaks when needed. Find moments to recharge during networking events or activities, such as stepping outside for a few minutes or finding a quiet space for reflection.
- Engage in pre-networking preparation. Research the attendees or topics beforehand so you can feel more comfortable and confident in your conversations.

Steps to Freedom from the Fear

1. Seek Support: Share your fears and concerns with a trusted friend, mentor, or coach. Discussing your anxieties with someone who understands can provide valuable insights, encouragement, and practical advice to help you overcome them.

2. Practice Visualization and Positive Affirmations: Visualize successful networking interactions and positive outcomes. Use affirmations or positive self-talk to boost your confidence and reframe any negative thoughts or self-doubt. Repeat statements such as "I am confident in my networking abilities" or "I am capable of building meaningful connections."

3. Take Small Steps: Start with small, low-pressure networking opportunities to build your confidence gradually. Attend local meetups or industry-specific events, join online communities or forums, or reach out to individuals within your existing network for informal conversations. Celebrate each small success to reinforce positive experiences.

NETWORKING SUCCESS

4. Attend Networking Workshops or Training: Participate in workshops or training sessions focused on networking skills. These sessions often provide valuable insights, strategies, and opportunities to practice networking in a supportive environment. Learning from experts and engaging in role-playing exercises can boost your confidence and refine your approach.

5. Reflect on Past Networking Successes: Recall and analyze past successful networking experiences. Identify what worked well, the positive outcomes, and the skills you utilized. Remind yourself that you have been successful in networking before and that you have the ability to replicate that success.

6. Embrace a Growth Mindset: Adopt a growth mindset that views networking as a skill that can be developed with time and practice. Embrace challenges and setbacks as learning opportunities rather than failures. Recognize that even experienced networkers face fears and challenges but continue to grow and improve.

7. Engage in Self-Care: Prioritize self-care to manage stress and anxiety associated with networking. Get enough rest, exercise regularly, eat healthily, and engage in activities that bring you joy and relaxation. Taking care of your well-being enhances your overall confidence and resilience.

8. Role Model Successful Networkers: Identify individuals who excel at networking and observe their behaviors and approaches. Analyze their strategies, communication style, and confidence levels. Model their positive attributes and adapt them to your own networking style.

9. Focus on Learning and Curiosity: Shift your mindset from solely seeking outcomes to a focus on learning and curiosity. Approach networking as an opportunity to learn from others, gain new perspectives, and expand your knowledge. Embrace the process rather than fixating solely on the end results.

10. Celebrate Progress: Acknowledge and celebrate your progress in overcoming fears and stepping outside your comfort zone. Each step forward, no matter how small, deserves recognition and celebration. This positive reinforcement reinforces your courage and motivates you to continue pushing past your fears.

Remember, everyone experiences fears and insecurities when it comes to networking. Embrace them as normal and treat them as opportunities for personal growth. With patience, practice, and a positive mindset, you can overcome your fears and become a more confident and effective networker.

The key is to step out of your comfort zone, take small steps, and practice consistently. As you face your fears head-on, you'll gradually build confidence and expand your network in meaningful ways.

Overcoming these fears takes a lot of practice and persistence. Gradually exposing yourself to networking situations, setting realistic goals, and focusing on building meaningful connections can help you grow more comfortable and confident in your networking abilities. Remember, everyone has fears, but with time and effort, they can be overcome.

Personality Types

While networking, you are likely to encounter individuals with various personality types, both positive and negative. Here are some common personality types you may come across while networking and tips on how to deal with them:

1. The Connector:
The Connector is highly sociable, outgoing, and skilled at making introductions. They have an extensive network and enjoy connecting with people. They are valuable contacts who can introduce you to new opportunities and influential individuals. To benefit from their networking skills, express your interests and goals clearly, and ask for introductions or recommendations.

2. The Expert:
The Expert is knowledgeable and experienced in their field. They have deep insights and can provide valuable advice and guidance. Engage with them by asking thoughtful questions, showing genuine interest in their expertise, and

seeking their insights. Acknowledge and appreciate their expertise, as it will help build a meaningful relationship.

3. The Listener:
The Listener is an attentive and empathetic individual who genuinely cares about others. They are great at active listening and making you feel heard. Take advantage of their listening skills by sharing your thoughts, challenges, and aspirations. They can provide valuable feedback, emotional support, and offer a different perspective on your situation.

4. The Mentor:
The Mentor is an experienced professional who is willing to share their knowledge and provide guidance. They can offer career advice, help you navigate challenges, and provide valuable insights. Approach them with respect and humility, express your interest in learning from them, and be open to their feedback and suggestions.

5. The Influencer:
The Influencer is a charismatic individual with a strong presence and a wide sphere of influence. They have the power to sway opinions and make things happen. Connect with them by demonstrating your enthusiasm for their work, expressing your admiration for their accomplishments, and finding common ground. Seek their advice and insights and show genuine interest in their opinions.

6. The Gatekeeper:
The Gatekeeper holds a position of authority or influence within an organization or industry. They have the power to grant access to valuable resources, opportunities, or connections. When interacting with a Gatekeeper, be respectful, professional, and demonstrate your value proposition. Clearly communicate how your skills, experience, or ideas can benefit their organization or network.

7. The Innovator:
The Innovator is a forward-thinking individual who is constantly seeking new ideas and solutions. They are often creative, open-minded, and willing to take risks. Connect with them by sharing your innovative ideas, demonstrating your passion for pushing boundaries, and engaging in thought-provoking discussions. Be receptive to their ideas and contributions, as they value intellectual stimulation.

8. The Connector #2:
The Connector is similar to the social Connector mentioned earlier, but in this context, they may be individuals who excel at leveraging technology or social

media platforms for networking. They have a strong online presence and are skilled at using digital tools to connect people. Engage with them by actively participating in relevant online communities, sharing valuable content, and leveraging technology to expand your network.

9. The Mentor-Protégé:
The Mentor-Protégé dynamic involves an experienced individual taking an active interest in mentoring and guiding a less experienced professional. If you come across someone who shows signs of being a mentor, express your interest in learning from them and seek their guidance. Be receptive to their feedback, actively implement their advice, and demonstrate your commitment to growth and development.

10. The Collaborator:
The Collaborator is someone who values teamwork and thrives on joint projects and partnerships. They are open to collaboration and seek opportunities to work together with others. Connect with them by expressing your interest in collaborative endeavors, sharing your skills and expertise that complement theirs, and exploring ways to work together on projects or initiatives.

11. The Thought Leader:
The Thought Leader is an influential individual who is respected for their expertise and insights in a specific field or industry. They may be authors, speakers, or recognized experts. Engage with them by attending their presentations or workshops, reading their publications, and actively participating in discussions or forums where they share their knowledge. Show genuine interest in their ideas and contribute to the conversation with thoughtful insights.

12. The Analytical Thinker:
The Analytical Thinker is detail-oriented, logical, and focused on data and facts. When engaging with them, be prepared to provide evidence and rationale to support your ideas or proposals. Use logical arguments and present information in a structured and organized manner. Be patient and open to discussing their concerns or objections, as they appreciate thoroughness and accuracy.

13. The Relationship Builder:
The Relationship Builder is someone who values building deep and meaningful connections. They prioritize trust, rapport, and personal connections in their networking interactions. Engage with them by showing genuine interest in their personal life, hobbies, or passions. Take the time to establish a personal connection

before discussing professional matters. Be attentive, empathetic, and invest in nurturing the relationship over time.

14. The Visionary:
The Visionary is a big-picture thinker who is enthusiastic about new possibilities and future trends. They are often innovative, optimistic, and inspire others with their vision. When networking with a Visionary, align your conversations with their overarching goals and aspirations. Share your ideas for the future, discuss emerging trends, and explore opportunities for collaboration that align with their vision.

15. The Diplomat:
The Diplomat is skilled at building and maintaining harmonious relationships. They are diplomatic, tactful, and excel in navigating complex social dynamics. When interacting with a Diplomat, be respectful, considerate, and avoid controversial or sensitive topics. Show appreciation for their contributions, acknowledge their efforts, and demonstrate your willingness to collaborate and find common ground.

16. The Connector #3:
The Connector, in this context, refers to individuals who excel at connecting people within specific industries, organizations, or communities. They have extensive networks and can facilitate introductions. Engage with them by expressing your specific networking goals, such as finding mentors, exploring job opportunities, or seeking partnerships. Be clear about the type of connections you are looking for, and they can assist you in expanding your network.

17. The Resilient:
The Resilient individual demonstrates strong determination, perseverance, and the ability to bounce back from setbacks. They have overcome challenges and adversity and have valuable insights to share. Engage with them by showing admiration for their resilience and seeking their advice on overcoming obstacles or navigating difficult situations. Learn from their experiences and incorporate their wisdom into your own journey.

Now here is the naughty list. You need to understand the negative personality types even more so as they can derail your networking efforts if not dealt with properly.

1. The Disruptor:
The Disruptor is an individual who tends to disrupt conversations, monopolize discussions, or divert attention away from others. They may interrupt or dominate conversations, making it challenging for others to contribute or establish meaningful connections. When encountering a Disruptor, it's important to maintain your composure and assertively steer the conversation back on track. Politely interject when necessary and redirect the focus to other participants.

2. The Infiltrator:
The Infiltrator is someone who attends networking events or gatherings with ulterior motives or hidden agendas. They may use manipulative tactics or exploit connections for personal gain without reciprocating the support or adding value to others. When dealing with an Infiltrator, trust your instincts and be cautious about sharing sensitive information. Focus on building relationships with individuals who genuinely value mutual support and collaboration.

3. The Gatekeeper:
The Gatekeeper, mentioned earlier as a positive personality type, can also exhibit negative traits. In this context, a negative Gatekeeper is someone who intentionally restricts access to valuable resources, opportunities, or connections. They may withhold information or deliberately limit networking opportunities for personal gain or to maintain a position of power. Dealing with a negative Gatekeeper can be challenging. In such cases, it's essential to explore alternative avenues for networking, seek support from other contacts, or leverage online platforms to expand your network.

4. The Self-Promoter:
The Self-Promoter is an individual who primarily focuses on self-promotion and constantly seeks attention or validation. They may dominate conversations by constantly talking about their achievements, experiences, or skills, without showing genuine interest in others. When interacting with a Self-Promoter, it's important to navigate the conversation tactfully. Find opportunities to redirect the discussion to more balanced and inclusive topics or seek out other individuals who are more receptive to building mutually beneficial relationships.

5. The Unreliable:

The Unreliable individual is someone who consistently fails to follow through on commitments or promises made during networking interactions. They may make empty promises, cancel meetings at the last minute, or consistently fail to deliver on their commitments. Dealing with an Unreliable contact can be frustrating and may waste your time and efforts. It's important to assess the situation objectively and consider redirecting your energy toward more reliable and trustworthy individuals.

6. The Taker:

The Taker is an individual who primarily focuses on what they can gain from networking interactions without offering much in return. They are often opportunistic and may only engage with others when they see a direct benefit for themselves. Dealing with a Taker can be challenging, as they may not contribute to a mutually beneficial relationship. It's important to be cautious and ensure that the networking exchange is balanced. Focus on building connections with individuals who demonstrate a willingness to give and support others.

7. The Negativist:

The Negativist is someone who constantly expresses negative opinions, complains, or brings a pessimistic attitude to networking conversations. They may undermine others' ideas or experiences and create a toxic atmosphere. When encountering a Negativist, it's important to maintain a positive mindset and not let their negativity affect your own motivation or enthusiasm. Politely redirect the conversation to more constructive topics or seek out individuals who bring a positive energy to networking interactions.

8. The Faker:

The Faker is an individual who presents a false image or exaggerates their accomplishments, skills, or connections. They may fabricate stories or pretend to have knowledge or expertise they don't possess. Dealing with a Faker can be challenging, as it can be difficult to determine the authenticity of their claims. It's important to trust your instincts and verify information when possible. Focus on building relationships with individuals who demonstrate honesty and transparency.

9. The Disinterested:

The Disinterested individual is someone who lacks genuine interest or enthusiasm in networking interactions. They may appear bored, disengaged, or distracted during conversations. Dealing with a Disinterested contact can be discouraging, but it's important not to take it personally. Instead, focus your efforts on individuals who show genuine interest and actively participate in networking exchanges.

10. The Opportunist:

The Opportunist is an individual who primarily seeks networking interactions for personal gain or to exploit others for their own benefit. They may engage in manipulative tactics, such as using flattery or false promises, to achieve their objectives. When dealing with an Opportunist, it's important to be cautious and maintain healthy boundaries. Focus on building relationships with individuals who demonstrate integrity, mutual respect, and a genuine interest in fostering meaningful connections.

11. The Dominator:

The Dominator is an individual who tends to assert dominance in networking interactions. They may interrupt or talk over others, monopolize conversations, and disregard the input or opinions of others. Dealing with a Dominator can be challenging, as they may hinder open and collaborative discussions. When interacting with a Dominator, it's important to assert yourself and ensure that your voice is heard. Politely interrupt if necessary and steer the conversation towards a more balanced and inclusive exchange of ideas.

12. The Egotist:

The Egotist is someone who constantly talks about themselves, their achievements, and their interests without showing genuine interest in others. They may dismiss or downplay the contributions of others and focus solely on self-promotion. Dealing with an Egotist requires patience and tact. Redirect the conversation to more balanced topics, actively listen to their perspectives, and find opportunities to highlight the contributions of others in the discussion.

13. The Critic:

The Critic is an individual who tends to be overly critical and judgmental in networking interactions. They may offer unsolicited negative feedback, undermine the ideas or accomplishments of others, or engage in nitpicking. Dealing with a Critic can be challenging, as their negative comments can impact confidence and motivation. It's important to remember that constructive feedback is valuable, but if the criticism is unwarranted or unhelpful, politely steer the conversation towards more positive and supportive discussions.

14. The Non-Engager:
A Non-Engager is someone who lacks active participation and engagement in networking interactions. They may be passive, unresponsive, or disinterested, making it difficult to establish meaningful connections. When encountering a Non-Engager, it's important to gauge their level of interest and adjust your approach accordingly. If their disinterest persists, it may be more beneficial to redirect your efforts towards individuals who are more open and responsive to networking exchanges.

15. The Gossip:
The Gossip is an individual who tends to engage in idle talk, spreading rumors, or discussing sensitive or private information about others. They may create a negative and toxic atmosphere in networking settings. When dealing with gossip, it's important to maintain professionalism and avoid engaging in or encouraging gossip. Focus on building relationships with individuals who value confidentiality, respect, and positive interactions.

16. The Negative Naysayer:
The Negative Naysayer tends to be pessimistic, critical, or dismissive. They may discourage your ideas or downplay your aspirations. It's important not to let their negativity affect you. Stay focused on your goals and maintain a positive attitude. Politely acknowledge their viewpoint but don't let it deter you from pursuing your objectives.

17. The Taker:
The Taker is primarily interested in what they can gain from networking interactions. They may be self-centered and less likely to offer support or reciprocate. Be cautious when engaging with them and set clear boundaries. Focus on building relationships with individuals who are genuinely interested in mutual support and collaboration.

18. Practice Emotional Intelligence:
Developing emotional intelligence can help you navigate challenging networking situations. It involves being aware of your own emotions and recognizing the emotions of others. By practicing empathy, active listening, and self-regulation, you can better understand the motivations and needs of negative personalities and respond in a more constructive manner.

19. Seek Support from Peers:

Connect with fellow networkers or colleagues who may have encountered similar negative personalities. Share your experiences, seek advice, and learn from their strategies for dealing with challenging individuals. Having a support system can provide you with valuable insights and encouragement when faced with difficult networking encounters.

20. Focus on Solutions, Not Problems:
Instead of dwelling on the negative behavior or personalities you encounter, focus on finding solutions and opportunities. Shift your mindset to one of problem-solving and forward-thinking. By focusing on solutions, you can maintain a positive outlook and proactively seek out individuals who can contribute to your networking goals.

21. Develop Conflict Resolution Skills:
Negative networking encounters may involve conflicts or disagreements. Developing conflict resolution skills can help you address conflicts in a constructive and productive manner. Learn techniques for active listening, understanding different perspectives, and finding common ground. Practice open communication and negotiation to find mutually beneficial resolutions.

22. Learn to Disengage:
In some cases, it may be necessary to disengage from a negative networking personality if the interactions consistently prove unproductive or toxic. Recognize when it's time to redirect your efforts elsewhere and focus on building relationships with individuals who align with your values and contribute positively to your network.

23. Maintain a Growth Mindset:
Adopt a growth mindset, which focuses on continuous learning and improvement. Embrace challenges as opportunities for growth and development. View negative networking personalities as learning experiences that can enhance your resilience, adaptability, and interpersonal skills. With a growth mindset, you can approach networking with a positive and proactive attitude.

24. Lead by Example:
Set a positive example in your networking interactions. Be respectful, supportive, and approachable. Show genuine interest in others and actively listen to their ideas and experiences. By leading by example, you can create a positive networking environment and inspire others to engage in constructive interactions.

25. Celebrate Positive Networking Experiences:
Acknowledge and celebrate the positive networking experiences you encounter. Whether it's a successful collaboration, a meaningful connection, or a supportive interaction, recognizing the positive aspects of networking can help counterbalance any negative encounters. Celebrate your achievements and the relationships you've built to stay motivated and engaged in the networking process.

When dealing with different personality types while networking, keep these general tips in mind:

- Be authentic: Be yourself and maintain authenticity in your interactions. People appreciate genuine connections and are more likely to respond positively when they sense sincerity.

- Listen actively: Practice active listening to understand others' perspectives and show genuine interest in their stories and experiences. This helps build rapport and fosters stronger connections.

- Offer value: Seek ways to provide value to others. Share your knowledge, offer assistance, and make introductions when appropriate. By being helpful, you establish yourself as a valuable contact in others' networks.

- Maintain professionalism: Present yourself professionally, demonstrate respect, and maintain a positive attitude. Treat others with courtesy and follow through on commitments. Professionalism helps build trust and enhances your reputation.

- Follow up: After networking events or meetings, follow up with individuals you connected with. Send personalized messages, express appreciation for the conversation, and explore opportunities for further collaboration or communication.

Dealing with negative personality types while networking requires a combination of assertiveness, discernment, and maintaining a positive mindset. It's important to remember that not every networking interaction will be fruitful or positive. By recognizing and minimizing interactions with negative personality types, you can prioritize building relationships with individuals who align with your values, offer genuine support, and contribute to a mutually beneficial network.

When encountering negative personality types while networking, it's crucial to remain professional, maintain your boundaries, and focus on building relationships with individuals who align with your values and goals. It's also helpful to surround yourself with a supportive network of contacts who can provide guidance and advice on navigating challenging situations. Remember that networking is a dynamic process, and not every interaction will be positive.

In dealing with different personality types while networking, it's essential to approach each interaction with an open mind, respect, and a willingness to learn from others. Adapt your communication style, actively listen, and be sensitive to their needs and preferences. Building effective relationships requires patience, empathy, and a genuine desire to connect with others. By leveraging the strengths of different personality types and navigating potential challenges with tact and grace, you can build a diverse and valuable network of connections.

Remember that networking is a two-way street, and building strong relationships takes time and effort. By adapting your approach to different personality types and maintaining a positive and proactive mindset, you can navigate the networking landscape effectively and build a valuable network of contacts.

Dealing with the Negative Types Effectively

Dealing effectively with negative networking personalities can be challenging, but here are some strategies to help you navigate those situations:

1. Maintain Professionalism:
Regardless of the negative behavior exhibited by others, it's important to maintain your professionalism. Stay calm, composed, and focused on your networking goals. Avoid getting drawn into arguments or confrontations, as it can detract from your own networking objectives.

2. Set Boundaries:
Establish clear boundaries for yourself and communicate your boundaries assertively. If someone is exhibiting negative behavior, politely and firmly let them know your expectations. For example, if someone is being overly critical or disrespectful, you can say, "I prefer constructive and positive conversations. Let's focus on finding common ground and exploring opportunities."

3. Stay Positive:
Maintain a positive attitude and mindset throughout networking interaction. Negativity can be contagious, so strive to bring a positive energy to the conversation. Redirect the discussion to more constructive topics, share success stories, or express gratitude for the opportunity to connect.

4. Listen Actively:
Even when dealing with negative personalities, practice active listening. Give them an opportunity to express their viewpoints, concerns, or grievances. By actively listening, you may gain insights into their motivations or underlying issues, which can help you navigate the conversation more effectively.

5. Don't Take It Personally:
Remember that the negative behavior of others is not a reflection of your worth or capabilities. It's important not to take their actions or comments personally. Maintain your self-confidence and focus on your own networking goals and objectives.

6. Seek Common Ground:
Look for areas of common interest or shared goals to redirect the conversation. Find topics that can foster a more positive and engaging exchange. By focusing on shared interests, you can create a more productive and constructive networking experience.

7. Limit Engagement:
If a negative personality continues to exhibit disruptive or toxic behavior despite your efforts, consider limiting your engagement with them. It's essential to prioritize your time and energy on individuals who are more receptive, supportive, and align with your networking goals.

8. Surround Yourself with Positive Influences:
Build a strong support network of positive and supportive individuals who can uplift you and provide guidance. Seek out mentors, colleagues, or friends who can offer advice on dealing with negative personalities and share strategies for overcoming challenges.

9. Learn from the Experience:
Every networking interaction, whether positive or negative, provides an opportunity for growth and learning. Reflect on the encounter and identify what you can learn from it. Consider how you can improve your own networking skills and strategies to navigate similar situations more effectively in the future.

10. Empathy and Understanding:
Try to understand the underlying reasons behind the negative behavior. Negative personalities may be dealing with personal challenges, insecurities, or other issues that contribute to their behavior. Practicing empathy can help you approach the situation with compassion and patience, which may help diffuse tension and open the door for more productive conversations.

11. Redirect the Conversation:
If you find yourself in a conversation dominated by negativity or unproductive behavior, redirect the conversation to a more positive and constructive topic. Introduce a relevant industry trend, ask for their insights on a particular challenge, or share a success story. By steering the conversation in a new direction, you can shift the focus away from negativity and encourage a more productive exchange.

12. Find Common Ground:
Look for shared interests, values, or goals with a negative personality. Finding common ground can help establish a connection and create a more harmonious conversation. Identify areas of mutual interest and build upon them to foster a more positive and collaborative interaction.

13. Maintain Confidence:
Negative personalities may try to undermine your confidence or make you doubt your abilities. It's essential to maintain your self-confidence and belief in your own worth. Remind yourself of your strengths, accomplishments, and the value you bring to the networking table. By staying confident, you can navigate challenging conversations more effectively.

14. Practice Assertiveness:
When faced with negativity or disruptive behavior, practice assertiveness. Clearly communicate your boundaries, expectations, and concerns. Express yourself respectfully but firmly. Use "I" statements to express how their behavior is impacting you and request a change in their approach. For example, you can say, "I would appreciate it if we could focus on positive and constructive conversations that benefit both of us."

15. Network Selectively:
Be selective in choosing the networking opportunities and events you attend. Research and seek out events or groups where you are more likely to encounter positive and like-minded individuals. By networking in environments that align with your values and interests, you can increase the chances of meeting individuals who are supportive and uplifting.

16. Practice Self-Care:
Dealing with negative networking personalities can be draining. It's important to prioritize self-care and take care of your own well-being. Engage in activities that recharge you, such as exercise, hobbies, spending time with loved ones, or practicing mindfulness. Taking care of yourself will help you maintain a positive mindset and approach networking interactions with resilience.

17. Reflect and Learn:
After encountering negative networking personalities, take the time to reflect on the experience. Consider what you can learn from the situation and how you can grow as a result. Reflect on your own reactions and determine if there are areas

where you can improve your own networking skills. Each encounter, positive or negative, can provide valuable lessons for personal and professional growth.

18. Practice Emotional Intelligence:
Developing emotional intelligence can help you navigate challenging networking situations. It involves being aware of your own emotions and recognizing the emotions of others. By practicing empathy, active listening, and self-regulation, you can better understand the motivations and needs of negative personalities and respond in a more constructive manner.

19. Seek Support from Peers:
Connect with fellow networkers or colleagues who may have encountered similar negative personalities. Share your experiences, seek advice, and learn from their strategies for dealing with challenging individuals. Having a support system can provide you with valuable insights and encouragement when faced with difficult networking encounters.

20. Focus on Solutions, Not Problems:
Instead of dwelling on the negative behavior or personalities you encounter, focus on finding solutions and opportunities. Shift your mindset to one of problem-solving and forward-thinking. By focusing on solutions, you can maintain a positive outlook and proactively seek out individuals who can contribute to your networking goals.

21. Develop Conflict Resolution Skills:
Negative networking encounters may involve conflicts or disagreements. Developing conflict resolution skills can help you address conflicts in a constructive and productive manner. Learn techniques for active listening, understanding different perspectives, and finding common ground. Practice open communication and negotiation to find mutually beneficial resolutions.

22. Learn to Disengage:
In some cases, it may be necessary to disengage from a negative networking personality if the interactions consistently prove unproductive or toxic. Recognize when it's time to redirect your efforts elsewhere and focus on building relationships with individuals who align with your values and contribute positively to your network.

NETWORKING SUCCESS

23. Maintain a Growth Mindset:
Adopt a growth mindset, which focuses on continuous learning and improvement. Embrace challenges as opportunities for growth and development. View negative networking personalities as learning experiences that can enhance your resilience, adaptability, and interpersonal skills. With a growth mindset, you can approach networking with a positive and proactive attitude.

24. Lead by Example:
Set a positive example in your networking interactions. Be respectful, supportive, and approachable. Show genuine interest in others and actively listen to their ideas and experiences. By leading by example, you can create a positive networking environment and inspire others to engage in constructive interactions.

25. Celebrate Positive Networking Experiences:
Acknowledge and celebrate the positive networking experiences you encounter. Whether it's a successful collaboration, a meaningful connection, or a supportive interaction, recognizing the positive aspects of networking can help counterbalance any negative encounters. Celebrate your achievements and the relationships you've built to stay motivated and engaged in the networking process.

Effective networking involves a combination of skills, mindset, and resilience. You can navigate negative networking personalities more effectively and create a network of individuals who contribute positively to your personal and professional growth.

By implementing these strategies, you can minimize their impact on your networking experience. Remember, the goal is to build meaningful connections and foster positive relationships, so prioritize your energy on individuals who contribute to your personal and professional growth.

While it's important to be open and receptive to networking opportunities, it's equally crucial to prioritize your well-being and protect yourself from negative influences. Focus on building relationships with individuals who are supportive, positive, and aligned with your values and goals.

How to Benefit from the Positive Personalities

Benefiting from positive networking personalities can significantly contribute to increasing your net worth and overall success. Here's how you can leverage these relationships for your advantage:

1. Build Strong Relationships:
Developing genuine and meaningful connections with positive networking personalities is key. Invest time and effort in cultivating these relationships by engaging in regular communication, showing support and interest in their endeavors, and offering assistance when appropriate. Building strong relationships allows for mutual trust, respect, and collaboration, which can lead to valuable opportunities.

2. Seek Mentorship and Guidance:
Positive networking personalities often possess valuable knowledge and experience. Take advantage of their expertise by seeking mentorship and guidance. They can provide insights, advice, and guidance on various aspects of your personal and professional development. Mentors can offer valuable feedback, introduce you to relevant contacts, and help you navigate challenges more effectively.

3. Collaborate on Projects:
Engage in collaborative projects with individuals who have a positive networking attitude. Collaborations allow you to leverage each other's skills, expertise, and networks. By combining resources and efforts, you can tackle more significant projects, expand your reach, and increase your chances of success.

4. Exchange Knowledge and Ideas:
Positive networking personalities are often open to sharing knowledge and ideas. Take advantage of this by engaging in intellectual discussions, attending industry events together, or participating in knowledge-sharing platforms. By exchanging insights and perspectives, you can broaden your horizons, gain new insights, and stay updated on the latest trends and innovations.

5. Gain Access to Opportunities:
Positive networking personalities are well-connected and may have access to valuable opportunities. These opportunities can range from job openings, partnerships, investment opportunities, speaking engagements, or industry events.

By nurturing relationships with individuals who have a positive networking influence, you increase your chances of being exposed to such opportunities.

6. Enhance Your Reputation:
Positive networking personalities can vouch for your skills, character, and credibility. When they speak positively about you, it enhances your reputation within your professional network. This can lead to increased trust and credibility among potential clients, partners, or employers, ultimately boosting your net worth.

7. Expand Your Network:
Positive networking personalities have their own networks that you can tap into. By building relationships with them, you gain access to their contacts and connections. This expands your network and opens up new avenues for collaboration, partnerships, and opportunities. Actively engage with the contacts they introduce you to and leverage these connections to further expand your reach and increase your net worth.

8. Support and Collaboration:
Positive networking personalities are likely to offer support and collaboration when you need it. They can provide recommendations, referrals, endorsements, or testimonials that enhance your professional profile. This support can significantly impact your career advancement, business growth, or personal brand, leading to increased net worth.

9. Stay Motivated and Inspired:
Surrounding yourself with positive networking personalities can keep you motivated and inspired. They can serve as role models, providing you with examples of success, resilience, and determination. Their stories and achievements can inspire you to push your boundaries, set higher goals, and strive for greater success, ultimately leading to an increase in your net worth.

10. Gain Industry Insights:
Positive networking personalities often have in-depth knowledge of the industry or field they operate in. Engage in conversations with them to gain valuable insights and stay updated on industry trends, challenges, and opportunities. This knowledge can help you make informed decisions, identify emerging market trends, and position yourself strategically within your industry.

11. Develop Partnerships:
Collaborating with positive networking personalities can lead to mutually beneficial partnerships. Identify individuals whose skills, expertise, or resources complement your own, and explore opportunities for collaboration. Partnering with like-minded professionals can enhance your offerings, expand your market reach, and lead to increased profitability and net worth.

12. Access Funding and Investment Opportunities:
Positive networking personalities may have access to funding sources or investment opportunities. They can introduce you to potential investors, venture capitalists, or angel investors who can provide the financial resources needed to grow your business or pursue new ventures. Their recommendations and endorsements can increase your credibility and attract potential investors.

13. Increase Referrals and Recommendations:
Positive networking personalities who believe in your capabilities are more likely to refer you to others or recommend your services. Their endorsements can result in new clients, customers, or business opportunities. Encourage satisfied clients and collaborators to provide testimonials or referrals that highlight the value you bring, thus increasing your net worth.

14. Improve Personal and Professional Development:
Engaging with positive networking personalities can contribute to your personal and professional growth. Attend workshops, seminars, or conferences where they share their expertise. Participate in skill-sharing sessions or take advantage of mentorship opportunities they offer. By investing in your development, you enhance your knowledge, skills, and overall market value.

15. Expand Geographical Reach:
Positive networking personalities often have connections in various geographic regions. By building relationships with them, you can tap into new markets and expand your geographical reach. They can provide insights into local business practices, cultural nuances, and market dynamics, giving you a competitive edge and increasing your potential customer base.

16. Collaborative Marketing and Promotions:
Partnering with positive networking personalities allows you to engage in collaborative marketing and promotions. By combining resources, you can create joint marketing campaigns, co-host events, or cross-promote each other's products

or services. Collaborative marketing efforts amplify your reach, attract a broader audience, and potentially lead to increased sales and revenue.

17. Access to Industry Influencers:
Positive networking personalities often have connections with industry influencers, thought leaders, or prominent figures. Through their networks, you can gain access to influential individuals who can amplify your brand, endorse your expertise, or provide opportunities for media exposure. Leveraging these relationships can significantly impact your visibility and net worth.

18. Develop Long-Term Relationships:
Building lasting relationships with positive networking personalities is crucial for sustained success. Focus on nurturing these connections by staying in touch, providing support, and maintaining a genuine interest in their success. Long-term relationships can lead to ongoing collaborations, referrals, and mutual growth, increasing your net worth over time.

The key to benefiting from positive networking personalities is to approach these relationships with authenticity, integrity, and a genuine desire to create value for both parties. Actively engage in networking events, industry gatherings, and online communities where you can connect with like-minded individuals. By building a strong network of positive personalities, you can leverage their knowledge, support, and opportunities to increase your net worth and achieve long-term success.

Focus on building mutually beneficial connections, supporting others, and maintaining a positive networking attitude yourself. By nurturing these relationships, you can create a strong network that propels your success and increases your net worth over time.

Remember, effective networking involves a combination of skills, mindset, and resilience. By applying these strategies, you can navigate negative networking personalities more effectively and create a network of individuals who contribute positively to your personal and professional growth.

Principles of Networking

Principles of Networking (Interpersonal Networking):

1. Building genuine relationships: Networking is about building authentic relationships with others. Understanding their needs, goals, and aspirations, and providing value and support are key elements in developing these relationships. Building genuine connections forms the foundation for long-term networking success.

2. Practicing reciprocity: Reciprocity involves giving and receiving within a networking context. By offering help, resources, or support to others without expecting immediate returns, you build goodwill and foster a mutually beneficial relationship. Practicing reciprocity often leads to opportunities and collaborations as others reciprocate your efforts.

3. Being proactive and consistent: Effective networking requires proactive and consistent effort. Taking the initiative to reach out, attending networking events, and staying connected with your network are vital for success. Being consistent in your interactions and following up regularly helps maintain strong relationships.

4. Being a good listener: Being an attentive listener is a crucial networking skill. It shows genuine interest in others' perspectives, challenges, and goals. Actively listening allows you to understand their needs better and identify ways to offer support or value.

5. Providing value and support: Networking is not just about what you can gain; it's also about what you can contribute. Offering assistance, sharing resources or knowledge, and providing support to others in your network helps establish yourself as a valuable and reliable connection.

6. Being open-minded and respectful: Networking involves connecting with individuals from diverse backgrounds, cultures, and perspectives. Being open-minded and respectful fosters a positive and inclusive networking environment. Embracing diversity enriches your network and opens doors to new opportunities.

7. Seeking mutual benefits: Networking should be a mutually beneficial exchange. Identifying ways to collaborate, create win-win situations, and mutually support

each other's goals strengthens the relationships within your network. By seeking mutual benefits, you establish a foundation of trust and goodwill.

8. Cultivating a diverse network: A diverse network brings together individuals from various industries, professions, and backgrounds. It provides access to different perspectives, knowledge, and opportunities. Actively seeking diversity in your network expands your reach and enhances your networking effectiveness.

9. Following up and staying connected: Following up after an initial meeting or interaction is crucial for maintaining and nurturing relationships. Sending personalized messages, scheduling follow-up meetings, or sharing relevant resources help you stay connected and top of mind with your network contacts.

10. Giving before receiving: Networking is not solely about asking for favors or opportunities. Prioritize giving and supporting others before expecting something in return. By being generous with your time, expertise, or resources, you build trust and goodwill, creating a reciprocal environment.

11. Embracing serendipity: Serendipity refers to the occurrence of valuable and unexpected connections or opportunities through chance or luck. Embracing serendipity means being open to unplanned encounters and seizing unexpected networking opportunities. Attend events outside of your usual circles, strike up conversations with new people, and be open to exploring diverse avenues. Serendipitous connections can lead to remarkable collaborations and opportunities that may not have been anticipated.

12. Leveraging social media and online platforms: In today's digital age, social media and online platforms play a significant role in networking. Utilize platforms like LinkedIn, Twitter, and industry-specific forums to connect with professionals in your field and engage in discussions. Share valuable content, contribute to relevant conversations, and actively participate in online communities. Leverage the power of these platforms to expand your network globally and showcase your expertise.

13. Nurturing dormant ties: Dormant ties refer to connections that have become inactive or less frequently engaged over time. While it's important to build new relationships, don't overlook the value of dormant ties. Reconnect with individuals you haven't interacted with in a while. Reach out, share updates on your professional journey, and express genuine interest in their lives. Reviving dormant

ties can reignite opportunities, unlock new connections, and tap into valuable resources.

14. Building an advisory board: An advisory board consists of a group of trusted individuals who provide guidance, support, and expertise in specific areas of your professional life. These individuals can be mentors, industry experts, or experienced professionals who can offer insights and advice. Establishing an advisory board helps you access diverse perspectives, tap into collective wisdom, and receive valuable input on critical decisions and challenges.

15. Participating in collaborative projects: Collaborative projects offer opportunities to connect with professionals across different disciplines and industries. Engaging in joint ventures, partnerships, or volunteer initiatives allows you to work alongside others, leverage complementary skills, and build lasting relationships. Collaborative projects foster teamwork, broaden your network, and create shared accomplishments that can open doors to new opportunities.

16. Paying it forward: Paying it forward involves proactively helping others without expecting anything in return. Actively seek ways to support and promote others in your network. Make introductions, provide recommendations, share resources, or offer mentorship to those who can benefit from your expertise and connections. Paying it forward not only strengthens your relationships but also cultivates a culture of reciprocity and goodwill within your network.

17. Cultivating a diverse network: Building a diverse network is essential for gaining fresh perspectives and broadening your horizons. Seek out individuals from different industries, backgrounds, cultures, and age groups. Engage with people who possess diverse skill sets, experiences, and viewpoints. A diverse network enhances creativity, fosters innovation, and exposes you to a wide range of opportunities and ideas.

18. Creating a personal brand: Developing a strong personal brand is an important principle of networking. Your personal brand represents your unique skills, expertise, and values. Define your professional identity and consistently communicate it across various channels, both online and offline. Build a reputation for yourself as someone who is knowledgeable, trustworthy, and reliable. Your personal brand can attract like-minded professionals and create opportunities for collaboration and growth.

NETWORKING SUCCESS

19. Engaging in active networking: Active networking involves being proactive and intentional in your networking efforts. It means actively seeking out opportunities to connect with others, such as attending industry events, joining professional associations, or participating in workshops and conferences. Actively engage in conversations, initiate introductions, and follow up with individuals you meet. By being proactive, you increase your chances of building valuable relationships and expanding your network.

20. Balancing online and offline networking: Networking can occur both online and offline, and it's important to strike a balance between the two. While online platforms provide convenience and reach, in-person interactions offer a deeper level of connection and rapport. Attend networking events, conferences, or seminars to meet professionals face-to-face and build stronger relationships. Combine online networking tools with in-person meetings to maximize your networking potential.

21. Fostering a culture of collaboration: Collaboration is a powerful networking principle that involves working together with others towards common goals. Actively seek opportunities to collaborate with individuals in your network on projects, initiatives, or joint ventures. Collaborative efforts not only strengthen relationships but also showcase your ability to work well with others and produce valuable outcomes.

22. Continual learning and self-development: Networking is not just about connecting with others but also about personal growth. Invest in your own development by continuously learning and acquiring new skills. Attend workshops, enroll in courses, read industry publications, and engage in professional development activities. By expanding your knowledge and expertise, you become a more valuable and influential networker.

23. Authenticity and vulnerability: Authenticity and vulnerability play a crucial role in building deeper connections with others. Be genuine and transparent in your interactions, sharing both your successes and challenges. Allow others to see your true self, as it fosters trust and authenticity in your relationships. When you show vulnerability, you create an environment that encourages others to open up and share their own experiences and insights.

24. Being a connector: Actively take on the role of a connector within your network. Identify opportunities where you can connect individuals who would benefit from knowing each other. Introduce professionals with complementary

skills or interests, facilitate collaborations, and share relevant resources. By being a connector, you add value to your network and position yourself as a trusted resource and hub of valuable connections.

25. Engaging in active listening: Active listening is a vital principle of effective networking. Practice active listening by giving your full attention to the person you are engaging with. Focus on understanding their perspective, ideas, and needs. Demonstrate empathy, ask follow-up questions, and provide thoughtful responses. Active listening shows respect and genuine interest, leading to deeper connections and meaningful conversations.

26. Being a resource and adding value: Networking is not just about what you can gain; it's also about what you can offer. Be a resource to others by sharing your knowledge, expertise, and resources. Provide valuable insights, offer assistance when needed, and be generous with your time and support. By adding value to others' lives and work, you build trust and strengthen your relationships.

27. Building a diverse range of relationships: Networking should go beyond building relationships solely with peers or those in similar roles. Seek to build connections with individuals at different stages of their careers, from various industries, and with diverse backgrounds. Engaging with a diverse range of people exposes you to new ideas, perspectives, and opportunities that can enrich your network and broaden your own horizons.

28. Establishing a reputation for reliability: Being reliable and trustworthy is crucial for networking success. Honor your commitments, follow through on promises, and meet deadlines. By establishing a reputation for reliability, you build credibility within your network. Others will be more likely to refer you to opportunities and collaborate with you if they perceive you as dependable and trustworthy.

29. Leveraging technology tools and platforms: Leverage technology tools and platforms to enhance your networking efforts. Utilize professional networking platforms such as LinkedIn to connect with professionals in your industry, join relevant groups, and showcase your expertise. Use email, video conferencing, or messaging apps to stay in touch with your network and engage in virtual networking opportunities. Embrace technological advancements that can facilitate efficient and effective networking.

Networking Success

30. Give without expecting immediate returns: Networking should not be solely transactional. While it's natural to expect some benefits from networking, focus on providing value without expecting immediate returns. Be generous with your time, expertise, and resources. The genuine act of giving fosters stronger relationships and can lead to unexpected opportunities and rewards in the long run.

31. Adaptability and flexibility: Networking principles should adapt to different contexts and situations. Recognize that networking is not a one-size-fits-all approach. Tailor your networking strategies based on the specific circumstances, goals, and preferences of the individuals you are connecting with. Be flexible in your approach and adapt to different networking styles and environments.

32. Maintaining a positive and supportive mindset: Networking can sometimes be challenging, but maintaining a positive and supportive mindset is essential. Embrace a mindset of abundance, where you believe that there are ample opportunities for everyone to succeed. Celebrate the achievements of others in your network, offer encouragement during setbacks, and provide support when needed. A positive and supportive mindset fosters a nurturing and collaborative networking environment.

33. Seeking feedback and self-improvement: Actively seek feedback from trusted individuals in your network. Request input on your skills, presentation, or networking strategies. Be open to constructive criticism and use it as an opportunity for self-improvement. Reflect on your networking experiences, identify areas for growth, and continuously refine your networking approach.

These principles, when applied effectively, contribute to the establishment of resilient, secure, and high-performing relationships that enable seamless interpersonal connectivity and support the diverse needs of the modern world.

The Rules of Engagement in Networking

When it comes to networking, there are certain guidelines or "rules of engagement" that can help you navigate interactions with others in a productive and respectful manner. Here are some detailed rules to consider:

1. Be Genuine and Authentic: Authenticity is key to building meaningful connections. Be yourself and let your true personality shine through. Avoid trying to impress or be someone you're not. People appreciate authenticity and are more likely to connect with you on a deeper level when they sense your genuineness.

2. Listen actively: Actively listening to others shows that you value their perspectives and opinions. Give your full attention, maintain eye contact, and refrain from interrupting. Ask thoughtful questions to demonstrate your interest and engage in meaningful conversations. Listening attentively helps build rapport and fosters a sense of connection.

3. Show Respect and Courtesy: Treat everyone you meet with respect and courtesy, regardless of their status or position. Be mindful of cultural differences and be open to learning from others' experiences. Use polite language, exhibit good manners, and be sensitive to others' boundaries and comfort levels.

4. Offer Value and Support: Seek opportunities to provide value and support to others in your network. Offer assistance, share relevant resources or information, and provide introductions when appropriate. By contributing positively to others' goals and aspirations, you strengthen the foundation of your relationships and foster a collaborative environment.

5. Follow Up Promptly: When you exchange contact information or make commitments, follow up promptly. Send a personalized email or message expressing your appreciation for the connection and reiterate any agreed-upon actions. This shows your professionalism and reliability, and it helps keep the momentum of the relationship going.

6. Maintain a Positive Attitude: Approach networking with a positive mindset and maintain an optimistic attitude. Be enthusiastic about meeting new people and exploring potential opportunities. Positivity is contagious and can attract others to connect with you. Even in challenging situations, strive to find the silver lining and focus on constructive solutions.

NETWORKING SUCCESS

7. Respect Privacy and Confidentiality: Networking often involves sharing personal or professional information. Respect the privacy and confidentiality of others by not sharing sensitive details without permission. Build trust by honoring confidentiality agreements and demonstrating discretion in your interactions.

8. Be Mindful of Time: Time is valuable for everyone involved in networking. Be punctual for meetings or events and respect others' schedules. During conversations, be mindful of the time and ensure that you are not monopolizing the conversation or overstaying your welcome. Being considerate of others' time demonstrates your professionalism and respect for their commitments.

9. Follow Professional Etiquette: Adhere to professional etiquette standards when networking. Dress appropriately for the occasion, use proper language and tone, and avoid controversial or offensive topics. Practice good hygiene and maintain a professional demeanor in your interactions. These small details contribute to creating a favorable impression.

10. Build and Maintain Relationships: Networking is not just about collecting business cards or making initial connections. It's about building and nurturing relationships over time. Follow up regularly, engage in meaningful conversations, and find ways to stay connected with individuals in your network. Remember to offer your support and celebrate their successes, reinforcing the mutual benefits of the relationship.

11. Be a Connector: Act as a connector within your network by introducing individuals who could benefit from knowing each other. Look for opportunities to facilitate connections and create value for others. By being a connector, you position yourself as a valuable resource and strengthen your relationships with both parties involved.

12. Practice Reciprocity: Networking is a two-way street. Be willing to give as much as you receive. Offer your support, expertise, and resources without expecting immediate returns. When others help you, express your gratitude and look for ways to reciprocate in the future. Building a culture of reciprocity strengthens the bonds within your network.

13. Embrace Diversity and Inclusion: Be open to engaging with individuals from diverse backgrounds, cultures, and perspectives. Embrace inclusivity by seeking out diverse viewpoints and actively creating an environment where everyone feels

welcome and valued. Networking with people who bring different experiences and insights can broaden your horizons and lead to innovative collaborations.

14. Continuously Learn and Grow: Networking provides opportunities for learning and personal growth. Stay curious and seek out new knowledge and skills related to your industry or field of interest. Attend workshops, webinars, or conferences, and engage in continuous learning to stay up to date with industry trends. By demonstrating a commitment to growth, you enhance your value within your network.

15. Practice Empathy and Emotional Intelligence: Develop empathy and emotional intelligence to better understand and connect with others. Put yourself in their shoes, be sensitive to their emotions, and respond with empathy. Emotional intelligence helps you navigate networking situations with tact, kindness, and understanding, which fosters stronger relationships.

16. Be Open to Feedback: Welcome feedback from others in your network and be open to constructive criticism. Feedback can help you improve your networking skills and refine your approach. Actively seek input from trusted contacts and be receptive to their suggestions. Incorporating feedback demonstrates your commitment to growth and development.

17. Be Gracious in Rejection: In networking, not every connection will lead to a fruitful outcome. Be gracious and respectful even when declining an opportunity or politely disengaging from a connection. Respond with gratitude for their interest and express that it may not align with your current goals or priorities. Maintain professionalism and leave the door open for future interactions.

18. Stay Connected through Social Media: Utilize social media platforms to stay connected with your network. Engage in relevant discussions, share valuable content, and celebrate the achievements of others. Social media provides an avenue to extend your reach and maintain visibility within your network. Use these platforms strategically to nurture relationships.

19. Seek Mentors and Role Models: Look for mentors and role models within your network who can guide and inspire you. Seek their advice, learn from their experiences, and observe their networking techniques. Mentors can offer valuable insights and help you navigate the challenges and opportunities that come with networking.

NETWORKING SUCCESS

20. Stay Persistent and Resilient: Networking requires persistence and resilience. Not every interaction will result in an immediate benefit, but with perseverance, you can build strong connections over time. Stay resilient in the face of setbacks or rejections and maintain a positive attitude. The right opportunities and connections will come with patience and persistence.

21. Be a Good Communicator: Effective communication is crucial in networking. Clearly articulate your thoughts, ideas, and goals. Be concise, yet engaging, in your conversations. Pay attention to your non-verbal cues, such as body language and tone of voice, to convey confidence and approachability. Good communication skills help you build rapport and establish meaningful connections.

22. Be Proactive: Take initiative in your networking efforts. Don't wait for opportunities to come to you; actively seek them out. Attend industry events, join professional associations, and engage in online communities. Initiate conversations, reach out to new contacts, and propose collaborations. Proactivity demonstrates your commitment and eagerness to expand your network.

23. Develop a Personal Brand: Define and cultivate your personal brand within your industry or field. Identify your unique strengths, skills, and values, and consistently align your actions and interactions with your brand. Be known for your expertise and reliability. A strong personal brand enhances your credibility and attracts others who resonate with your values.

24. Be a Problem Solver: Networking is not only about making connections but also about providing solutions. Listen attentively to the challenges and needs of others and offer your expertise and support whenever possible. By being a problem solver, you position yourself as a valuable resource within your network that builds trust and credibility.

25. Foster Long-Term Relationships: Aim for building long-term relationships rather than focusing solely on short-term gains. Invest time and effort in nurturing and maintaining connections. Show a genuine interest in others' success, provide ongoing support, and celebrate their achievements. Long-term relationships have the potential to bring ongoing opportunities and collaborations.

26. Stay Updated and Relevant: Keep yourself updated with the latest trends, advancements, and news in your industry. Attend workshops, read industry publications, and engage in continuous learning. Being knowledgeable and staying

relevant positions you as a valuable asset within your network and allows you to contribute meaningful insights and ideas.

27. Be Mindful of Social Dynamics: Understand the social dynamics within your network and adapt accordingly. Be aware of power dynamics, hierarchies, and cultural nuances. Treat everyone with respect and avoid making assumptions based on appearances or titles. Being mindful of social dynamics helps you navigate networking situations with sensitivity and professionalism.

28. Give and Receive Feedback: Actively seek feedback from trusted contacts within your network. Welcome constructive criticism as an opportunity for growth and improvement. Similarly, offer feedback when appropriate, providing valuable insights to help others enhance their skills and performance. A culture of feedback strengthens relationships and contributes to individual and collective growth.

29. Embrace Continuous Learning: Approach networking with a growth mindset and a commitment to continuous learning. Be open to new ideas, perspectives, and ways of doing things. Attend workshops, seminars, and webinars to expand your knowledge and skills. The more you learn, the more valuable you become to your network.

30. Stay Grateful and Express Appreciation: Show gratitude and appreciation for the connections and opportunities you receive through networking. Acknowledge the support, guidance, and contributions of others. Send thank-you notes, express your appreciation in person, or find other meaningful ways to show your gratitude. Gratitude fosters goodwill and strengthens your network relationships.

Remember, these rules of engagement are meant to guide your networking efforts and help you navigate interactions in a meaningful and effective way. By incorporating these principles into your networking approach, you can build a strong network, foster meaningful connections, and open doors to exciting opportunities for personal and professional growth.

By following these additional rules of engagement, expand your network, and make the most of your networking efforts. Remember that networking is a long-term investment, and by consistently applying these principles, you can build a valuable and supportive network that contributes to your personal and professional success.

Creating a Strong Network

Creating a strong network that propels your success and increases your net worth over time requires a strategic and intentional approach. Here are the steps to help you build a robust network:

1. Define Your Networking Goals:
Start by clarifying your networking goals. Determine what you hope to achieve through your network, whether it's finding business opportunities, expanding your knowledge, seeking mentorship, or advancing your career. Defining your goals helps you focus your efforts and make targeted connections.

2. Identify Your Target Audience:
Identify the individuals or groups who are most likely to help you achieve your networking goals. Consider industry professionals, thought leaders, potential clients, mentors, or colleagues who share similar interests or work in complementary fields. Narrowing down your target audience helps you prioritize your networking efforts and build meaningful connections.

3. Build an Online Presence:
Establish a strong online presence through platforms like LinkedIn, professional websites, or social media channels. Optimize your profiles to highlight your skills, expertise, and accomplishments. Share valuable content, engage in industry discussions, and connect with relevant individuals. An impressive online presence increases your visibility and attracts like-minded professionals to your network.

4. Attend Industry Events and Networking Functions:
Actively participate in industry events, conferences, seminars, and networking functions. These gatherings provide opportunities to meet professionals from various backgrounds, share ideas, and establish connections. Prepare in advance by researching speakers, attendees, and topics to maximize your engagement during these events.

5. Engage in Active Listening:
Develop active listening skills to foster meaningful conversations. Show genuine interest in others, ask open-ended questions, and actively listen to their responses. Focus on building connections based on shared interests, experiences, or goals. By

demonstrating that you value and understand others' perspectives, you create a solid foundation for long-term relationships.

6. Provide Value and Support:
Offer value and support to others without expecting immediate returns. Share your knowledge, insights, and resources to help others solve problems or achieve their goals. Act as a resource, connector, or mentor whenever possible. By providing value, you position yourself as a trusted and reliable network member, increasing the likelihood of reciprocation in the future.

7. Follow Up and Nurture Relationships:
After making initial connections, follow up with individuals to strengthen relationships. Send personalized messages, express gratitude, and offer continued support. Stay in touch through regular communication, whether it's meeting for coffee, attending industry events together, or exchanging ideas through online platforms. Consistent nurturing of relationships ensures they remain active and mutually beneficial.

8. Seek Mentors and Advisors:
Identify potential mentors and advisors who can guide you in your professional journey. Look for individuals who have achieved success in your desired field or possess expertise that aligns with your goals. Approach them with respect and humility, clearly articulate what you hope to gain from the mentorship and be receptive to their guidance and feedback.

9. Join Professional Associations and Groups:
Engage in professional associations, industry-specific groups, or online communities. These platforms provide opportunities to connect with like-minded professionals, share knowledge, and access resources. Actively participate in discussions, contribute valuable insights, and build relationships with key individuals within these networks.

10. Maintain a Long-Term Perspective:
Networking is not a one-time event but an ongoing process. Maintain a long-term perspective and invest in building lasting relationships. Regularly evaluate your network, identify areas for growth, and seek opportunities to expand your connections. Adapt your networking strategy as your goals and circumstances evolve, ensuring that your network continues to support your growth and success.

Building a strong network takes time, effort, and genuine engagement. Be patient, persistent, and authentic in your interactions. Focus on cultivating relationships based on mutual respect, trust, and support. By following these steps and nurturing your network consistently, you can build a strong dependable network.

Working the Room

Working a room effectively for networking purposes involves a strategic approach to engage with multiple individuals and make meaningful connections. Here are some steps to help you work a room successfully:

1. Set Clear Goals: Before entering the room, clarify your networking goals. Determine what you hope to achieve, whether it's making a specific number of connections, finding potential collaborators, or gaining insights into a particular industry. Setting clear goals helps you stay focused and maximizes your networking efforts.

2. Research and Prepare: If possible, gather information about the event, attendees, or key speakers in advance. This knowledge allows you to initiate conversations more easily and engage with others on relevant topics. Prepare a few conversation starters or questions to break the ice and facilitate meaningful discussions.

3. Approach with Confidence: Walk into the room with confidence and a positive attitude. Maintain an open posture, make eye contact, and wear a genuine smile. Projecting confidence and approachability attracts others and makes it easier for them to approach you.

4. Start with Small Groups: Look for smaller groups of people engaged in conversations rather than trying to approach larger clusters. Smaller groups tend to be more welcoming and easier to join. Approach the group politely, listen for a moment to get a sense of the discussion, and then find an opportunity to introduce yourself and contribute to the conversation.

5. Be a Good Listener: When engaging in conversations, practice active listening. Pay attention to what others are saying, show genuine interest, and ask follow-up questions to demonstrate your engagement. Listening attentively allows you to understand the needs and interests of others, making it easier to find common ground and establish a connection.

6. Introduce Yourself Effectively: When introducing yourself, be concise and engaging. Share your name, a brief summary of your background or expertise, and your current focus or goals. Craft an elevator pitch that highlights your unique value proposition and leaves a lasting impression.

NETWORKING SUCCESS

7. Show Genuine Interest: Networking is not just about talking about yourself; it's about building relationships. Show genuine interest in others by asking open-ended questions about their work, interests, or challenges. Actively listen to their responses and find opportunities to offer support or share relevant insights.

8. Exchange Business Cards or Contact Information: Be prepared with your business cards or a digital means of exchanging contact information. When you feel a connection is worth pursuing further, offer your card or ask for theirs. Make a note on the back of the card to remember key details about the person and the context of your conversation.

9. Connect with Confidence: After the event, follow up with the individuals you are connected with. Send personalized emails or messages referencing your conversation and expressing your interest in staying in touch. Take the initiative to schedule follow-up meetings or calls to deepen the relationship.

10. Build Relationships Beyond the Event: Networking is an ongoing process, so it's important to nurture relationships beyond the initial meeting. Stay in touch through social media platforms, attend industry events together, or offer support and assistance when needed. Building long-term relationships contributes to a robust network.

11. Be Respectful of Time: While it's essential to engage in conversations, be mindful of time constraints. Avoid monopolizing someone's time and be aware of signals that indicate the conversation should come to a close. Respect others' schedules and gracefully move on to connect with other individuals.

12. Follow Up with Event Organizers: If you found the event valuable, consider reaching out to the event organizers to express your appreciation. Provide feedback on what you enjoyed and offer suggestions for improvement. Building relationships with event organizers can lead to future opportunities and increased visibility within your industry.

13. Be Mindful of Body Language: Pay attention to your body language as it can significantly impact how others perceive you. Maintain an open posture, avoid crossing your arms, and stand or sit confidently. Make eye contact with others to show attentiveness and interest. Positive and approachable body language can attract others and make it easier for them to engage with you.

14. Be Present and Engaged: When interacting with others, be fully present in the conversation. Avoid distractions like checking your phone or scanning the room. Give your undivided attention to the person you're speaking with, actively listen to their words, and respond thoughtfully. This level of engagement demonstrates respect and genuine interest.

15. Be Authentic: Authenticity is key in networking. Be true to yourself and let your genuine personality shine through. Avoid trying to impress others with exaggerated stories or adopting a false persona. People are more likely to connect with you when they sense authenticity and sincerity.

16. Practice Effective Follow-Up: After the event, make it a priority to follow up with the individuals you met. Send personalized emails or messages within a day or two, referencing your conversation and expressing your interest in continuing the connection. Personalize your message by mentioning specific details from your discussion to help them remember the interaction.

17. Offer Value: Networking is not just about what you can gain; it's about offering value to others as well. Look for opportunities to provide assistance, share resources, or make introductions that could benefit the people you meet. By being a giver and adding value to others, you build a reputation as a helpful and trustworthy networker.

18. Practice Active Networking: Networking isn't limited to formal events. Make networking a part of your everyday life by actively seeking opportunities to connect with others. Attend industry conferences, workshops, and seminars. Join professional organizations or online communities. Engage in volunteer work or participate in social activities where you can meet new people and expand your network.

19. Seek Opportunities for Collaboration: Networking is not only about building connections but also about finding opportunities for collaboration. Look for synergies between your expertise and the skills of others you meet. Explore potential collaborations, joint projects, or partnerships that can benefit both parties. Collaboration can lead to shared success and a stronger network.

20. Be Patient and Persistent: Building a strong network takes time and effort. Don't expect immediate results or overnight success. Be patient and persistent in your networking endeavors. Follow up with contacts, maintain regular

communication, and consistently nurture your relationships. Over time, your network will grow, and opportunities will arise.

21. Reflect and Learn: After each networking event, take the time to reflect on your experiences and learn from them. Evaluate what worked well and what could be improved. Consider the types of connections you made, the conversations you had, and the insights you gained. Use this feedback to refine your networking approach and make adjustments for future events.

By applying these additional tips, you can enhance your networking skills and make the most out of every networking opportunity. Remember that networking is a continuous process, and building authentic and meaningful connections takes time. With practice, confidence, and a genuine desire to connect with others, you can develop a strong network that supports your personal and professional growth.

Remember, working a room effectively requires a balance between being proactive and genuine in your interactions. Focus on building relationships rather than merely collecting business cards and aim for quality connections over quantity. With practice and persistence, you can become adept at working a room and making meaningful connections that contribute to your personal and professional growth.

Step by Step Process

Here is a step-by-step process, along with specific places to go and actions to take, to start networking with others:

1. Set clear networking goals: Define your networking goals to give your efforts a clear direction. Determine what you want to achieve through networking, such as expanding your professional contacts, seeking career advice, or finding potential collaborators. Clarifying your goals will help you focus your efforts and measure your progress.

2. Research relevant networking events and organizations: Identify networking events, conferences, trade shows, and industry-specific organizations that align with your professional interests and goals. Research online platforms, such as Meetup or Eventbrite, or industry associations to find relevant events and organizations in your area or online.

3. Attend networking events and conferences: Start attending networking events and conferences related to your field. Dress professionally, bring business cards, and prepare a short elevator pitch that introduces yourself and your professional background. Actively engage in conversations, approach individuals or groups, and initiate meaningful discussions about common interests or industry trends.

4. Participate in workshops and seminars: Seek out workshops, seminars, and training sessions related to your industry. These events often provide opportunities for smaller group interactions and in-depth discussions. Actively participate, ask questions, and contribute your insights to demonstrate your knowledge and expertise.

5. Join professional associations and groups: Look for professional associations, industry-specific groups, or online communities related to your field. These platforms offer a space to connect with professionals sharing similar interests. Attend their meetings, join their online discussions, and contribute valuable insights. Actively engage with members by offering assistance, sharing resources, or participating in group projects.

6. Utilize online networking platforms: Leverage online networking platforms such as LinkedIn, Twitter, or industry-specific forums. Create a well-crafted and professional profile that showcases your skills, experience, and interests. Connect

with professionals in your industry, join relevant groups, and actively engage in discussions. Share valuable content, provide insights, and build relationships virtually.

7. Attend industry-related webinars and virtual events: In addition to in-person events, take advantage of virtual opportunities. Attend webinars, virtual conferences, and online panel discussions related to your industry. Participate actively by asking questions, contributing to the chat or Q&A sessions, and connecting with other participants through virtual networking features.

8. Engage in informational interviews: Reach out to professionals whose work or expertise aligns with your interests. Request informational interviews to learn more about their career paths, industry insights, and advice. Prepare thoughtful questions, actively listen during the interview, and express gratitude for their time and insights. These conversations can provide valuable connections and potential mentors.

9. Follow up and nurture relationships: After networking events or engaging with professionals, follow up with personalized messages or emails to express your appreciation and interest in maintaining contact. Share any relevant resources or articles that you discussed during your conversation. Stay connected by periodically checking in, sharing updates, or inviting individuals for virtual coffee meetings.

10. Give back and support others: Be proactive in offering support and assistance to others in your network. Share your expertise, offer introductions, or provide recommendations when appropriate. Actively promote and celebrate the achievements of others in your network. Being a valuable resource and supportive connection establishes you as a trusted and reliable professional.

11. Seek mentorship opportunities: Identify professionals in your field who have achieved the level of success you aspire to. Reach out to them and express your admiration for their work. Ask if they would be open to mentoring or providing guidance. A mentor can offer valuable insights, advice, and support as you navigate your career path.

12. Engage in volunteering or community activities: Participate in volunteering initiatives or community activities related to your interests or industry. This not only allows you to contribute to a cause you care about but also provides opportunities to meet like-minded individuals and expand your network.

Collaborating with others in a non-professional setting can foster genuine connections and open doors to new opportunities.

13. Attend alumni events: Connect with individuals from your alma mater by attending alumni events or joining alumni associations. These events often bring together professionals from various industries and offer opportunities to network with individuals who share a common educational background. Engage in conversations about shared experiences and leverage the alumni network for career opportunities.

14. Utilize existing connections: Tap into your existing network and leverage those connections to expand your reach. Inform friends, family, and colleagues about your networking goals and ask if they can introduce you to professionals in your desired field. Personal introductions can often lead to more meaningful and productive conversations.

15. Cultivate online presence and thought leadership: Establish yourself as a thought leader in your industry by sharing valuable content and insights online. Create a professional blog, contribute guest articles to industry publications, or start a podcast or YouTube channel. Consistently provide valuable information and engage with your audience, which can attract like-minded professionals and expand your network.

16. Attend industry-specific workshops and training programs: Identify industry-specific workshops, training programs, or boot camps that offer focused learning opportunities. Participate in these programs to acquire new skills, expand your knowledge, and connect with industry experts. Engaging with individuals who share your passion for professional growth can lead to valuable networking connections.

17. Engage in social or hobby-based groups: Explore social or hobby-based groups outside of your professional sphere. Participate in activities or join clubs related to your personal interests. Engaging with individuals in a relaxed and informal setting can lead to authentic connections and provide a refreshing break from traditional networking environments.

18. Establish an online portfolio or website: Create an online portfolio or website that showcases your work, projects, and achievements. This provides a centralized platform where potential connections can learn more about your expertise and accomplishments. Share the link to your portfolio or website when networking,

enabling others to gain a comprehensive understanding of your professional profile.

19. Attend industry-specific trade shows or exhibitions: Identify industry-specific trade shows, exhibitions, or conventions that attract professionals from your field. These events offer opportunities to learn about new trends, innovations, and products while connecting with industry leaders and peers. Engage in conversations with exhibitors, attend seminars, and exchange contact information with individuals who align with your professional goals.

20. Reflect, evaluate, and adjust: Regularly reflect on your networking efforts and evaluate their effectiveness. Consider the connections you've made, the opportunities that have arisen, and the impact on your professional growth. Assess what strategies have worked well and what areas can be improved. Adjust your approach accordingly to refine your networking efforts and maximize their impact.

21. Embrace diversity and inclusivity: Actively seek out diverse perspectives and connect with professionals from different backgrounds, cultures, and experiences. Embracing diversity and inclusivity in your network expands your horizons, promotes innovation, and allows you to tap into a broader range of knowledge and expertise.

22. Engage in cross-industry networking: Look beyond your immediate industry and connect with professionals in adjacent or complementary fields. Cross-industry networking exposes you to fresh ideas, alternative approaches, and potential collaborations that can lead to unique opportunities and insights.

23. Attend niche or specialized events: Explore niche or specialized events that cater to specific interests, industries, or technologies. These events offer the chance to connect with individuals who share a specific passion or focus, allowing for more in-depth and targeted conversations.

24. Seek out virtual networking opportunities: In addition to attending physical events, actively participate in virtual networking opportunities. Virtual conferences, webinars, online forums, and social media groups provide avenues to connect with professionals from around the world, overcoming geographical limitations and expanding your network globally.

25. Engage with thought leaders and influencers: Identify thought leaders, industry influencers, and prominent figures in your field. Follow their work, engage with

their content, and contribute thoughtful comments and insights. Engaging with thought leaders can raise your visibility within the industry and potentially lead to valuable connections and collaborations.

26. Leverage social media platforms strategically: Utilize social media platforms strategically for networking purposes. LinkedIn, Twitter, and even platforms like Instagram or TikTok can be valuable tools for connecting with professionals, showcasing your expertise, and engaging in industry discussions. Curate your online presence to align with your professional goals and actively engage with others in your network.

27. Establish a personal advisory board: Consider forming a personal advisory board consisting of trusted professionals from diverse backgrounds. These individuals can provide guidance, advice, and different perspectives on your professional journey. Regularly meet or connect with your advisory board members to seek their insights and tap into their collective wisdom.

28. Seek out networking opportunities during travel: If you frequently travel for work or leisure, leverage these opportunities to network with professionals in different locations. Research local industry events, meetups, or conferences happening during your visit. Networking with professionals from different regions can broaden your network and open doors to new possibilities.

29. Participate in online mastermind groups: Join online mastermind groups or communities that bring together professionals with similar goals or interests. These groups often provide a platform for focused discussions, problem-solving, and peer support. Engaging in a mastermind group allows you to tap into the collective knowledge and experiences of a select group of professionals.

30. Engage in reverse mentoring: Consider engaging in reverse mentoring, where you connect with professionals from younger generations or with different skill sets. Reverse mentoring allows for a knowledge exchange, where you can learn from their fresh perspectives, technological expertise, and understanding of emerging trends. This type of networking relationship can be mutually beneficial and foster innovation.

NETWORKING SUCCESS

Remember, networking is a dynamic and evolving process. Stay open to new opportunities, embrace emerging trends and technologies, and continuously seek ways to expand and diversify your network. By embracing these unique aspects, you can create a network that is vibrant, diverse, and supportive, enhancing your professional growth and opportunities.

By following these steps and taking action in various networking contexts, you can establish a strong foundation for building and expanding your professional network. Remember to be genuine, consistent, and focused on building meaningful connections based on mutual value and support. Networking is a continuous process, so embrace it as an ongoing part of your professional journey.

Networking is an ongoing process, so continue to attend events, engage in online discussions, and expand your connections over time. Be patient, genuine, and focused on building meaningful relationships. By following this step-by-step process and taking specific actions, you can effectively start networking with others and cultivate a strong professional network.

By following these principles, you can establish a robust network of connections that can provide support, opportunities,

Additional Tips and Tricks

Here are a few additional tips and tricks to enhance your networking effectiveness:

1. Set Clear Goals: Define specific goals for your networking efforts. Identify what you want to achieve, whether it's building connections in a particular industry, finding mentors, or exploring new career opportunities. Clear goals provide direction and motivation for your networking activities.

2. Develop Your Personal Brand: Cultivate a strong personal brand that reflects your expertise, values, and unique qualities. Clearly articulate your strengths, passions, and the value you bring to potential connections. Consistency in how you present yourself across different platforms and interactions helps create a strong and memorable impression.

3. Practice Active Referral Networking: Be proactive in referring and recommending others within your network. Actively look for opportunities to connect people who could benefit from knowing each other. This demonstrates your willingness to help and contributes to building a strong network where people are inclined to reciprocate.

4. Utilize Informational Interviews: Request informational interviews with professionals you admire or individuals in roles or industries you're interested in. These interviews provide an opportunity to learn from their experiences, gain insights, and potentially build a mentorship relationship. Prepare thoughtful questions and approach the interviews with a genuine desire to learn.

5. Embrace Diversity and Inclusion: Actively seek out diverse perspectives and actively engage with individuals from different backgrounds, industries, and cultures. Embracing diversity in your network broadens your horizons, exposes you to new ideas, and fosters creativity and innovation in your own work.

6. Volunteer and Give Back: Engage in volunteer work or community involvement related to your interests or industry. Not only does this contribute to a meaningful cause, but it also provides opportunities to connect with like-minded individuals who share your values and passions.

7. Be Generous with Your Knowledge: Share your knowledge, insights, and experiences with others. Offer assistance, provide valuable resources, and

participate in discussions and forums where you can contribute your expertise. Being generous and helpful positions you as a valuable resource and strengthens your network.

8. Follow Up and Nurture Relationships: Maintain regular contact with your network by following up and nurturing relationships over time. Send occasional emails, congratulate others on their achievements, and stay connected through social media. Show genuine interest and support for their endeavors, which helps foster long-term, mutually beneficial relationships.

9. Continuously Learn and Stay Informed: Stay updated on industry trends, news, and developments. Read relevant books, blogs, articles, and research papers to enhance your knowledge and have meaningful conversations with others. Being well-informed positions you as a knowledgeable and valuable network contact.

10. Reflect and Evaluate: Regularly assess the effectiveness of your networking efforts. Reflect on your experiences, successes, and challenges. Identify areas for improvement and adjust your strategies accordingly. Networking is a continuous process of learning and growth, so ongoing evaluation is key.

11. Authentic Listening: Active and authentic listening is a powerful tool in networking. When engaging in conversations, give your full attention to the person speaking. Practice empathetic listening, show genuine interest in their thoughts and experiences, and ask relevant questions. By being a good listener, you demonstrate respect and create a space for meaningful connections to flourish.

12. Mutual Support and Collaboration: Networking is not just about what you can gain but also about what you can contribute. Look for ways to support others in your network by sharing resources, providing assistance, and offering valuable insights. Actively seek opportunities for collaboration where both parties can benefit, fostering a mutually supportive network environment.

13. Continuous Relationship Nurturing: Networking is an ongoing process, and nurturing relationships is crucial. Stay connected with your network by regularly reaching out, whether through emails, phone calls, or in-person meetings. Show interest in their endeavors, celebrate their successes, and provide support when needed. Consistency in relationship-building efforts strengthens the bonds within your network.

14. Attend Networking Events and Conferences: Actively participate in industry-related events, conferences, and professional associations. These gatherings provide opportunities to meet new people, exchange ideas, and expand your network. Be proactive in engaging with attendees, introducing yourself, and initiating conversations. Look for opportunities to contribute through panel discussions, presentations, or workshops.

15. Online Networking: Leverage the power of online platforms and social media to extend your networking reach. Join professional groups and forums related to your field of interest. Engage in conversations, share valuable content, and connect with like-minded individuals. Online networking allows you to connect with people from diverse geographical locations and access a vast pool of knowledge and opportunities.

16. Mentorship and Mentoring Others: Seek out mentors who can provide guidance and support in your professional journey. A mentor can offer valuable insights, share experiences, and help expand your network. Additionally, consider becoming a mentor yourself, offering guidance to others who can benefit from your expertise. Mentoring relationships can deepen your connections and contribute to your personal and professional growth.

17. Follow Up and Follow Through: When you meet someone new or exchange contact information, remember to follow up and follow through on your commitments. Send a personalized email or message, express gratitude for the connection, and explore ways to continue the conversation. Consistent follow-up demonstrates your reliability and builds trust within your network.

18. Reflect and Learn: Take time to reflect on your networking experiences and learn from them. Identify what worked well and areas for improvement. Adapt your approach based on the feedback and lessons learned. Networking is a continuous learning process, and by embracing a growth mindset, you can refine your skills and make your networking efforts more effective.

Effective networking is about building meaningful connections, cultivating relationships, and creating a network of individuals who can support and inspire one another. By incorporating these tips and insights into your networking approach, you can enhance your networking skills, expand your opportunities, and create a strong and supportive network that contributes to your personal and professional success.

Utilizing these resources can help you expand your network, enhance your networking skills, and remain open to new opportunities. Be proactive, consistent, and authentic in your networking efforts, and always strive to build genuine connections based on mutual interests and shared values.

Going Global

In today's increasingly global world, effective networking strategies can help individuals navigate diverse cultural landscapes, expand their reach, and build connections across borders. Here are some effective strategies for networking in this context:

1. Leverage Social Media Platforms: Utilize social media platforms such as LinkedIn, Twitter, and professional online communities to connect with professionals from around the world. Actively engage in industry-specific groups, share valuable content, and participate in discussions to expand your network and establish yourself as a thought leader in your field.

2. Attend International Conferences and Events: Look for conferences, trade shows, or events that have an international focus or attract professionals from different countries. These gatherings provide excellent opportunities to meet

individuals from diverse backgrounds, exchange ideas, and forge global connections.

3. Engage in Cross-Cultural Communication: Develop cross-cultural communication skills to navigate and understand cultural nuances. Be respectful of different cultural norms, adapt your communication style, and demonstrate cultural sensitivity when interacting with individuals from different countries and backgrounds.

4. Join Global Networking Organizations: Seek out networking organizations that have a global presence or a focus on connecting professionals internationally. These organizations often provide networking events, webinars, and resources that facilitate connections and collaboration across borders.

5. Utilize Online Networking Platforms: Explore online networking platforms that specifically cater to global professionals. These platforms facilitate virtual networking, connecting individuals from different parts of the world based on shared interests, industries, or expertise.

6. Foster Relationships with Expatriate Communities: Connect with expatriate communities or organizations in your area or online. Expatriate communities often provide a supportive network of individuals who have experience navigating cross-cultural environments and can offer insights, advice, and networking opportunities.

7. Embrace Virtual Networking: Leverage virtual networking tools such as video conferencing, webinars, and virtual meetups to connect with professionals globally. Virtual networking eliminates geographical barriers and allows you to build connections with individuals from different countries without the need for in-person meetings.

8. Collaborate on Global Projects: Seek opportunities to collaborate on projects with professionals from different countries or participate in international initiatives. Engaging in global projects fosters cross-cultural understanding, expands your network, and enhances your professional reputation on a global scale.

9. Develop Language Skills: If possible, consider learning additional languages to facilitate communication with professionals from different countries. Language skills can help you build rapport, demonstrate cultural understanding, and navigate networking situations more effectively.

10. Seek Out Global Mentors: Identify mentors who have experience in global settings or have successfully built international networks. Their guidance and insights can provide valuable perspectives and help you navigate the challenges and opportunities of networking in a global context.

11. Participate in Virtual Conferences and Webinars: With the rise of virtual events, take advantage of attending international conferences and webinars. These platforms allow you to connect with professionals from around the world, engage in discussions, and expand your knowledge while building valuable connections.

12. Seek International Internships or Exchanges: Consider pursuing international internships or exchanges to gain firsthand experience in different cultural and professional contexts. These opportunities provide a unique chance to network with professionals from diverse backgrounds and establish global connections.

13. Engage in Global Volunteer Work: Engaging in volunteer work on a global scale can provide networking opportunities while making a positive impact. Join international organizations or initiatives that align with your interests or expertise, allowing you to connect with like-minded individuals from different countries.

14. Collaborate with Global Online Communities: Join online communities or forums that focus on specific industries or professional interests on a global scale. Actively participate in discussions, share insights, and collaborate with professionals from various parts of the world.

15. Conduct Informational Interviews: Reach out to professionals in your target industries or countries for informational interviews. These interviews allow you to learn about different markets, gain insights into cultural nuances, and build connections with individuals who can offer guidance and potential networking opportunities.

16. Engage in Thought Leadership: Establish yourself as a thought leader in your field by sharing valuable content, writing blog posts or articles, and participating in industry discussions. This positions you as an expert and attracts connections from around the world who value your insights and expertise.

17. Build Relationships with International Alumni Networks: Connect with alumni networks of universities or educational institutions with global reach. These

networks often have chapters or events in different countries, providing networking opportunities with professionals who share a common educational background.

18. Attend Global Business Expos and Trade Fairs: Explore international business expos and trade fairs relevant to your industry. These events bring together professionals, entrepreneurs, and businesses from various countries, offering opportunities for networking, collaboration, and exploring global markets.

19. Foster a Global Mindset: Cultivate a global mindset by staying informed about international affairs, trends, and economic developments. Being knowledgeable about global issues and having a broad perspective enhances your conversations, helps you build connections with individuals from different backgrounds, and positions you as a global-minded professional.

20. Engage in Cross-Cultural Mentorship: Seek cross-cultural mentorship opportunities, where you can learn from professionals from different countries or cultural backgrounds. A cross-cultural mentor can provide guidance, insights, and advice on navigating global networking and building connections across borders.

Remember that building a global network requires a genuine interest in different cultures, an open mindset, and a willingness to adapt to diverse environments. Embrace the diversity of perspectives and experiences that global networking offers and approach every interaction with curiosity and respect. By incorporating these strategies into your networking approach, you can effectively connect with professionals from around the world and leverage the opportunities of our increasingly globalized world.

Building a global network takes time, effort, and a genuine interest in connecting with individuals from diverse backgrounds. Be open-minded, curious, and respectful of different cultures and perspectives. By embracing these strategies, you can effectively expand your network and capitalize on the opportunities that today's increasingly global world offers.

Diversity & Networking

Adapting to a diversity of perspectives and diverse environments involves developing cultural intelligence, fostering empathy, and cultivating a mindset that embraces differences. Here are the steps to help you navigate this process in detail:

1. Educate Yourself: Begin by educating yourself about different cultures, customs, and perspectives. Read books, articles, and academic papers on intercultural communication, diversity, and inclusion. Take online courses or attend workshops that focus on cross-cultural understanding and communication.

2. Challenge Assumptions and Stereotypes: Acknowledge and challenge your own assumptions, biases, and stereotypes. Recognize that diversity encompasses more than just visible differences such as ethnicity or nationality, and that individuals from the same culture may have unique perspectives and experiences. Approach each interaction with an open mind and a willingness to learn.

3. Develop Cultural Intelligence: Cultivate cultural intelligence, which involves the ability to adapt and work effectively in diverse cultural contexts. This includes three components: cognitive (knowledge and understanding of different cultures), emotional (awareness and management of emotions in cross-cultural interactions), and behavioral (the ability to adjust behaviors to fit different cultural norms).

4. Practice Active Listening: Actively listen and seek to understand others' perspectives. Be present in conversations, ask open-ended questions, and show genuine interest in what others have to say. Practice empathy and put yourself in their shoes to gain a deeper understanding of their experiences and viewpoints.

5. Adapt Communication Styles: Adapt your communication style to fit the cultural norms and preferences of the individuals you interact with. Be mindful of different communication styles, directness levels, and non-verbal cues. Use clear and concise language, avoid slang or jargon that may be unfamiliar, and be sensitive to potential language barriers.

6. Embrace Different Communication Channels: Be open to utilizing different communication channels preferred in different cultures or environments. For example, some cultures may prioritize face-to-face interactions, while others may rely more on digital communication. Adapt your approach accordingly to ensure effective and respectful communication.

7. Cultivate Empathy: Cultivate empathy by seeking to understand others' experiences, challenges, and perspectives. Practice empathy by actively listening, validating their feelings, and showing empathy in your responses. This helps foster a sense of connection and mutual understanding across diverse perspectives.

8. Respect Cultural Differences: Respect and value cultural differences without judgment. Embrace the idea that different perspectives and approaches can lead to innovative solutions and opportunities for growth. Avoid making comparisons or assuming superiority or inferiority of certain cultures or viewpoints.

9. Be Open to Learning and Growth: Approach each cross-cultural interaction as an opportunity for learning and growth. Embrace the discomfort that may arise from encountering different perspectives, as it allows you to expand your understanding and challenge your own assumptions. Be open to feedback and be willing to adjust your own behaviors and perspectives when necessary.

10. Build Relationships: Build meaningful relationships with individuals from diverse backgrounds. Actively seek out networking opportunities with individuals who have different perspectives and experiences. Engage in conversations that go beyond surface-level interactions and invest time in building trust and mutual understanding.

11. Seek Feedback: Seek feedback from individuals with different perspectives to gain insights into how your words and actions are perceived. This feedback can help you refine your approach, deepen your understanding, and improve your ability to navigate diverse environments.

12. Practice Cultural Sensitivity: Demonstrate cultural sensitivity by being aware of cultural norms, traditions, and taboos. Be mindful of potential cultural differences in gestures, humor, or personal boundaries. When in doubt, observe and ask for guidance to ensure you navigate diverse environments respectfully.

Certainly! Here are a few more steps to adapt to a diversity of perspectives and diverse environments:

13. Embrace Cultural Humility: Cultivate a mindset of cultural humility, which involves recognizing the limits of your own cultural knowledge and being open to learning from others. Acknowledge that your perspective is just one among many, and approach interactions with a genuine desire to understand and learn from different cultures and perspectives.

14. Practice Flexibility and Adaptability: Be flexible and adaptable in your approach to different cultural contexts. Recognize that norms and expectations may vary across cultures, and be willing to adjust your behavior, communication style, and decision-making process accordingly. This demonstrates your respect for cultural differences and your willingness to adapt to diverse environments.

15. Seek Out Diversity in Your Network: Actively seek out and engage with individuals from diverse backgrounds in your personal and professional networks. Surrounding yourself with a diverse group of people exposes you to different perspectives, challenges your assumptions, and broadens your understanding of the world.

16. Collaborate on Cross-Cultural Projects: Engage in cross-cultural projects or initiatives that require collaboration with individuals from different backgrounds. Working together towards a common goal allows you to gain insights into different work styles, problem-solving approaches, and cultural values. Embrace the opportunity to learn from your colleagues and build strong cross-cultural relationships.

17. Develop Intercultural Conflict Resolution Skills: Conflict is a natural part of cross-cultural interactions. Invest in developing intercultural conflict resolution

skills, such as active listening, finding common ground, and seeking win-win solutions. Learn to navigate disagreements respectfully and constructively, recognizing that different perspectives can lead to innovative solutions.

18. Stay Curious and Ask Questions: Cultivate a curious mindset and ask questions to deepen your understanding of different cultures and perspectives. Avoid making assumptions or generalizations. Instead, show genuine interest in others' experiences, traditions, and values. Asking respectful questions demonstrates your willingness to learn and your respect for diverse viewpoints.

19. Practice Cultural Sensitivity in Body Language: Be mindful of cultural differences in body language and non-verbal communication. Gestures, eye contact, personal space, and physical touch can vary across cultures. Educate yourself about cultural norms to ensure that your body language aligns with the expectations of the cultural context you are in.

20. Reflect on Your Own Cultural Conditioning: Reflect on your own cultural conditioning and biases. Recognize that your upbringing, values, and beliefs may shape your perceptions and interactions. Regular self-reflection helps you become aware of any biases and allows you to challenge them, fostering more inclusive and respectful relationships.

21. Celebrate Diversity and Inclusion: Actively promote diversity and inclusion in your personal and professional spheres. Create opportunities for diverse voices to be heard, advocate for inclusive practices, and challenge exclusionary behaviors or policies. By fostering an inclusive environment, you encourage individuals to bring their authentic selves and contribute to a rich tapestry of perspectives.

22. Remain Open to Growth and Learning: Cultivate a growth mindset that embraces ongoing learning and personal development. Recognize that adapting to diverse perspectives and environments is a lifelong journey. Be open to feedback, seek continuous learning opportunities, and remain humble in the face of new knowledge and experiences.

Here are a few additional tips and considerations to further support your ability to adapt to a diversity of perspectives and diverse environments:

1. Be Mindful of Power Dynamics: Recognize and be sensitive to power dynamics that may exist in cross-cultural interactions. Be mindful of how your own privilege or position may influence the dynamics of the conversation or relationship. Strive for equitable and inclusive interactions where everyone's voices are heard and respected.

2. Seek Cultural Immersion Opportunities: Immerse yourself in different cultures through travel, study abroad programs, or cultural exchange initiatives. Direct exposure to different cultural contexts allows for a deeper understanding and appreciation of diverse perspectives.

3. Develop Resilience and Patience: Adapting to diverse perspectives and environments can be challenging at times. Develop resilience and patience to navigate misunderstandings, conflicts, and cultural differences. Embrace the learning process and view challenges as opportunities for personal growth.

4. Build Cross-Cultural Teamwork Skills: If you work in a multicultural team, invest in building cross-cultural teamwork skills. Foster a collaborative and inclusive team environment by promoting open communication, active listening, and valuing diverse contributions. Encourage team members to share their unique perspectives and create a safe space for open dialogue.

5. Stay Updated on Global Trends: Stay informed about global trends, socio-political developments, and current events. This knowledge helps you engage in meaningful conversations and understand the broader context in which diverse perspectives exist.

6. Foster Inclusive Leadership: If you are in a leadership position, model inclusive behaviors and create an inclusive work or community environment. Foster a culture where diverse perspectives are valued, and individuals feel safe to express their opinions and contribute their unique insights.

7. Cultivate a Growth Mindset: Embrace a growth mindset that allows you to embrace challenges and learn from them. See mistakes as opportunities for learning, and approach each experience with a sense of curiosity and willingness to improve.

8. Seek Support and Mentorship: Engage with mentors, coaches, or advisors who have experience in navigating diverse perspectives and environments. Their guidance and support can help you navigate challenges, offer insights, and provide a sounding board for your experiences.

9. Reflect on Your Own Biases Regularly: Regularly reflect on your own biases and cultural conditioning. Actively challenge any biases or prejudices that may hinder your ability to embrace diversity. Engage in self-reflection and seek opportunities for personal growth and transformation.

10. Contribute to Diversity Initiatives: Get involved in diversity and inclusion initiatives within your organization or community. Actively participate in activities or programs that promote cultural understanding, inclusivity, and equal opportunities for all.

Staying open to a diversity of perspectives and diverse environments is an ongoing journey that requires continuous learning, self-reflection, and openness. By embracing these additional tips and incorporating them into your interactions and experiences, you can foster an inclusive mindset, build meaningful connections, and thrive in diverse settings.

Adapting to a diversity of perspectives and diverse environments requires self-awareness, empathy, and a genuine willingness to learn from others. By practicing these steps, you can build strong connections, foster inclusive environments, and thrive in a world that celebrates diversity and cultural richness.

By embracing these steps and actively engaging with individuals from different backgrounds, you can foster meaningful connections, build cultural intelligence, and thrive in diverse environments.

Resources for Networking

To network more effectively and remain open to networking opportunities, there are various resources available that can help you expand your network and enhance your networking skills. Here are some detailed resources you can consider:

1. Professional Networking Websites: Utilize professional networking websites such as LinkedIn, which is a popular platform for professionals to connect, share insights, and discover new opportunities. Create a compelling and professional profile, actively engage in relevant groups and discussions, and use the platform's search features to find and connect with individuals in your field of interest.

2. Networking Events and Conferences: Attend industry-specific networking events, conferences, and trade shows relevant to your field. These events provide opportunities to meet professionals, exchange business cards, engage in discussions, and build relationships. Check online event platforms, industry associations, and local business organizations to find upcoming events in your area.

3. Alumni Networks: Leverage your alumni network from universities, colleges, or professional programs. Many educational institutions have alumni associations that organize networking events, mentorship programs, and online platforms for alumni to connect. Reach out to fellow alumni, participate in alumni events, and explore networking opportunities within your alma mater's community.

4. Professional Associations: Join professional associations and organizations related to your industry or area of interest. These associations often offer networking events, conferences, webinars, and online forums where you can connect with like-minded professionals, share insights, and stay updated on industry trends. Research and identify relevant associations in your field and become an active member.

5. Online Networking Platforms: Explore online networking platforms that focus on specific industries or professional interests. Examples include Meetup, Eventbrite, or industry-specific forums and communities. These platforms allow you to connect with professionals, join relevant groups, and participate in virtual events or discussions.

6. Online Courses and Webinars: Enroll in online courses or webinars that focus on networking skills, personal branding, or professional development. Platforms like Udemy, Coursera, and LinkedIn Learning offer a wide range of courses that can help you enhance your networking abilities, build confidence, and expand your knowledge base.

7. Business Incubators and Accelerators: Consider joining business incubators or accelerators that support startups and entrepreneurs. These programs often provide access to networking events, mentoring opportunities, and resources to help you connect with investors, industry experts, and potential collaborators.

8. Social Media: Leverage social media platforms strategically for networking. Apart from LinkedIn, platforms like Twitter, Facebook, and Instagram can be used to connect with professionals, industry influencers, and thought leaders. Engage in industry-related discussions, share valuable content, and use appropriate hashtags to expand your reach.

9. Professional Development Workshops: Attend professional development workshops and seminars that focus on networking skills, communication, and relationship building. These workshops provide practical tips, techniques, and

strategies to improve your networking abilities and maximize your interactions with others.

10. Business and Entrepreneurship Centers: Explore resources available at local business and entrepreneurship centers or hubs. These centers often host networking events, mentorship programs, and workshops designed to support professionals and entrepreneurs in building connections and fostering growth.

11. Networking Books and Publications: Read books and publications on networking, relationship building, and professional development. Some recommended titles include "Never Eat Alone" by Keith Ferrazzi, "How to Win Friends and Influence People" by Dale Carnegie, and "Give and Take" by Adam Grant. These books offer valuable insights, strategies, and stories to help you navigate the world of networking effectively.

12. Podcasts and Webcasts: Listen to podcasts and webcasts that focus on networking, entrepreneurship, and personal development. Many podcasts feature interviews with successful professionals and provide valuable insights and networking tips. Some notable podcasts include "The Tim Ferriss Show," "HBR IdeaCast," and "The School of Greatness."

Key Takeaways

Networking plays a pivotal role in various aspects of our lives. From career development and entrepreneurship to personal growth and community engagement, networking enables individuals to expand their horizons, tap into diverse perspectives, and access valuable resources. By building a strong network, individuals can gain support, mentorship, and opportunities that may not have been possible otherwise.

1. Knowledge Exchange: Networking facilitates the exchange of knowledge, ideas, and best practices. Engaging with individuals from different backgrounds and industries expands our intellectual horizons, fosters creativity, and stimulates innovative thinking.

2. Career Advancement: Networking is crucial for career growth and professional development. Building relationships with industry professionals, mentors, and potential employers can lead to job opportunities, promotions, and access to insider information.

3. Support and Mentorship: A robust network provides a support system that offers guidance, advice, and encouragement. Mentors within the network can offer insights, share experiences, and help navigate challenges.

4. Collaborations and Partnerships: Networking opens avenues for collaborations and partnerships. By connecting with like-minded individuals or organizations, individuals can explore joint projects, share resources, and amplify their impact.

To maximize the benefits of networking, individuals should employ effective strategies that enhance their networking abilities. Here are some key strategies to consider:

1. Define Your Networking Goals: Clearly define your networking goals to establish a sense of direction. Identify what you want to achieve through networking, such as expanding your industry connections, gaining specific knowledge, or finding potential collaborators.

2. Develop a Strong Personal Brand: Cultivate a strong personal brand that represents your unique skills, experiences, and values. Clearly communicate your strengths and value proposition to potential connections.

3. Be Authentic and Genuine: Approach networking with authenticity and a genuine desire to build meaningful connections. Show interest in others, actively listen, and find common ground for engagement.

4. Attend Networking Events: Attend industry conferences, seminars, and workshops to meet professionals from diverse backgrounds. Engage in conversations, ask thoughtful questions, and exchange contact information for future follow-ups.

5. Utilize Online Networking Platforms: Leverage online networking platforms such as LinkedIn, industry-specific forums, or virtual networking events. Maintain an updated profile, engage in relevant discussions, and connect with individuals of interest.

6. Volunteer and Engage in Professional Associations: Join professional associations or engage in volunteering activities related to your field. These opportunities provide a platform to connect with like-minded individuals and showcase your expertise.

7. Follow Up and Nurture Relationships: After networking interactions, follow up with individuals to express gratitude and reinforce the connection. Stay in touch through occasional emails, social media interactions, or in-person meetings to nurture relationships over time.

8. Give Back and Offer Value: Be proactive in providing value to your network. Share relevant resources, introduce connections, or offer assistance when

appropriate. By being a valuable resource, you strengthen relationships and enhance reciprocity within your network.

Ancient Sayings and Quotes about Networking

Ancient sayings, beliefs, and quotes about network and net worth reflect the wisdom and understanding of previous generations regarding the value of connections, relationships, and material wealth. While specific quotes or sayings directly addressing the term "network" or "net worth" may be rare in ancient texts, there are philosophical and spiritual teachings that convey related concepts. Here are some notable examples:

"Vasudhaiva Kutumbakam" (The world is one family)

This ancient Sanskrit saying from the Maha Upanishad emphasizes the interconnectedness of all beings. It conveys the idea that the entire world is a network of interconnected individuals and that we should treat everyone as part of our extended family.

"No man is an island"

Although not ancient in origin, this famous quote by John Donne, a 17th-century English poet, reflects the understanding that humans are inherently social beings and that we thrive through connections with others. It suggests that we are all part of a larger network of relationships.

"It's not what you know, but who you know"

This phrase, often attributed to various sources, highlights the belief that building a strong network of relationships is crucial for success in various aspects of life. It underscores the idea that connections and networking opportunities can open doors and create opportunities.

"A friend in need is a friend indeed"

This proverb, with roots in ancient wisdom, emphasizes the value of supportive relationships and connections. It suggests that true friends are those who stand by your side during difficult times, highlighting the importance of a strong support network.

"For where your treasure is, there your heart will be also"

This quote from the Bible, specifically Matthew 6:21, speaks to the concept of net worth. It emphasizes that one's true priorities and values are reflected in how they allocate their resources, both material and emotional. It suggests that our worth is tied to what we value and invest in.

"Great wealth is a great slavery"

This quote by Seneca, a Stoic philosopher from ancient Rome, conveys the understanding that excessive material wealth can become a burden. It reminds us that focusing solely on accumulating wealth may lead to a loss of freedom and a lack of true fulfillment.

"A rich man is not one who has the most but needs the least"

This saying highlights the distinction between material wealth and true contentment. It suggests that the worth of an individual should not be measured solely by their material possessions but by their ability to find satisfaction with what they have.

"Your network is your net worth"

While the origin of this quote is debated, it has gained popularity in recent times. It emphasizes the value of one's network and suggests that the relationships and connections we cultivate are instrumental in determining our overall worth and success in life.

"A chain is only as strong as its weakest link"

This proverb, often attributed to the philosopher Thomas Reid, emphasizes the importance of strong and reliable connections within a network. It implies that the overall effectiveness and worth of a network depend on the strength and quality of its individual members.

"In union, there is strength"

This quote, attributed to Aesop, an ancient Greek storyteller, highlights the power and value of collaboration and collective effort. It suggests that when individuals come together and work in harmony, their combined strength and capabilities increase, enhancing their overall worth and impact.

"Wealth consists not in having great possessions but in having few wants"

This quote by the Greek philosopher Epictetus emphasizes the idea that true wealth and worth lie in contentment and simplicity. It suggests that reducing one's desires and needs can lead to a greater sense of fulfillment and inner wealth, irrespective of material possessions.

"The best time to plant a tree was 20 years ago. The second best time is now"

While not directly related to networking or net worth, this ancient Chinese proverb highlights the importance of taking action and building connections in the present. It encourages individuals to seize opportunities and invest in relationships, recognizing that the benefits may be reaped in the future.

"A single thread of hope is stronger than all the chains that bind you"

This quote, often attributed to the American poet and author Joseph Addison, emphasizes the resilience and power of connections. It suggests that even a small network of supportive relationships and positive influences can have a profound impact on one's worth and ability to overcome challenges.

These ancient sayings, beliefs, and quotes offer timeless wisdom and insights into the significance of networking, relationships, and the true meaning of net worth. They remind us of the value of genuine connections, collaboration, and contentment as we navigate our personal and professional lives.

While these quotes and sayings may not explicitly mention "network" or "net worth," they offer insights into the significance of connections, relationships, and the pursuit of genuine worth in life. They stress the importance of balancing material wealth with meaningful connections and a sense of purpose.

Affirmations and Mantras Networking

Certainly! Mantras and affirmations can be powerful tools to build confidence and strengthen the will needed for effective networking and expanding one's network. Here are some examples:

1. "I am worthy of meaningful connections and valuable relationships."

This affirmation reminds you that you deserve to build connections and form relationships that bring value and fulfillment to your life. It reinforces your self-worth and encourages you to seek out meaningful networking opportunities.

2. "I am confident in my ability to connect with others and make a positive impact."

This mantra instills confidence in your networking abilities. It affirms that you have the skills and qualities to engage with others, make a positive impression, and create mutually beneficial relationships.

3. "I embrace new connections and opportunities with open arms and an open mind."

This affirmation encourages you to approach networking with openness and receptivity. It reminds you to be open-minded, willing to explore new possibilities, and receptive to different perspectives and opportunities that arise through networking.

4. "Every interaction is an opportunity for growth and connection."

This mantra reframes networking as a continuous journey of growth and learning. It reminds you to view every interaction, whether formal or informal, as a chance to expand your network, gain insights, and forge meaningful connections.

5. "I am a magnet for positive and supportive relationships."

This affirmation helps attract positive and supportive individuals into your network. It reinforces the belief that you naturally draw in like-minded individuals who contribute positively to your personal and professional growth.

6. "I confidently share my unique strengths and expertise with others."

This mantra encourages you to embrace and share your unique qualities, knowledge, and skills. It reminds you to have confidence in what you bring to the table, enabling you to make a genuine impact in your networking interactions.

7. "I approach networking with curiosity, compassion, and authenticity."

This affirmation encourages you to embody qualities that foster deeper connections. It reminds you to approach networking with genuine curiosity, empathy, and an authentic desire to understand and support others.

8. "I release any fear or self-doubt and step into my networking power."

This mantra helps you let go of fear and self-doubt that may hinder your networking efforts. It empowers you to overcome insecurities and step into your networking potential with confidence and determination.

9. "I am a magnet for meaningful connections and opportunities that align with my goals."

This affirmation focuses on attracting connections and opportunities that are aligned with your aspirations and objectives. It reinforces the belief that you are capable of attracting and nurturing relationships that contribute to your personal and professional growth.

10. "I embrace discomfort and step out of my comfort zone to expand my network."

This mantra encourages you to embrace discomfort and take bold steps outside your comfort zone. It reminds you that growth and expansion happen when you are willing to push your boundaries and seek out new networking experiences.

11. "I approach every networking event or situation with enthusiasm and a positive mindset."

This affirmation encourages you to approach networking events or situations with enthusiasm and a positive outlook. It reminds you to embrace each opportunity as a chance to connect with others and create meaningful relationships.

12. "I am a confident and engaging communicator, expressing myself with clarity and authenticity."

This mantra reinforces your communication skills and affirms that you are confident and engaging when interacting with others. It encourages you to express yourself authentically, fostering genuine connections.

13. "I am a giver in my network, offering support, insights, and value to others."

This affirmation reminds you of the importance of being a giver in your network. It emphasizes the value of offering support, sharing insights, and providing value to others, which in turn strengthens your network and builds reciprocal relationships.

14. "I am open to collaboration and partnerships that create mutual growth and success."

This mantra emphasizes the power of collaboration and partnerships in networking. It affirms your openness to collaborative opportunities and highlights the potential for mutual growth and success through shared endeavors.

15. "I release any attachment to the outcome and trust the process of networking."

This affirmation encourages you to let go of attachment to specific outcomes and trust in the organic process of networking. It reminds you to focus on building authentic connections and let opportunities unfold naturally.

Mantras and affirmations are most effective when personalized and aligned with your specific goals and values. Choose the ones that resonate with you and reflect your intentions for networking. Incorporate them into your daily routine through repetition, visualization, or journaling, and allow them to empower and guide you on your networking journey.

The effectiveness of mantras and affirmations lies in consistent practice and repetition. Choose the ones that resonate with you the most and integrate them into your daily routine. Repeat them with conviction and belief, allowing them to shape your mindset and strengthen your networking skills and confidence over time.

About The Author

Michelle Dornor, Founder & Owner, Dornor Consulting

Creator & Host of Pearls of Wisdom & Power Podcast

Michelle Dornor

Spiritual Advisor, Life & Business Strategist, & USAF Desert Storm Veteran

Michelle is the Founder of Dornor Consulting LLC, an advisory company that blends intuitive knowledge with strong analytical skills to bring a total solution to resolve reoccurring issues in personal life or business.

Dornor Consulting is also the parent company for her weekly online talk show Pearls of Wisdom & Power Transformation Room. The talk show currently has over 1000 members and is growing with over 200 people listening live on a weekly basis across multiple online platforms. The success of the Transformation Room led to Michelle starting a paid subscription service where she teaches success principles via live events such as her biweekly mastermind book club, esoteric movie night & discussion, and a live Q&A "Ask Michelle" where members can ask Michelle anything about business and life.

Michelle is also a four-time author when including this writing, with her third offering titled, Pearls of Wisdom & Power: Life Changing Lessons for Spiritual Advancement, making the Amazon Top 100 best seller list in 2 categories immediately following launch.

Michelle is currently a successful sales consultant with a well-known Fortune 500 technology company and has a proven track record of exceeding company sales goals and KPI's with a tenure of 13 years effective August 2023. In 2020, Michelle graduated Summa Cum Laude as an Honors Fellow with a GPA of 3.95 earning a double major bachelors in PR & Marketing. She was named to the Deans list over 20 times for her entire university tenure and is a member of three international honor societies and several professional organizations. Michelle also honorably served her country during the Desert Storm campaign as a service member of the United States Air Force.

When Michelle is not running her consulting company, growing her online community, working hard or hitting the books, you can find her traveling to international destinations with her wonderful husband of 14 years. Michelle also enjoys volunteering her time and resources to worthy causes that promote human prosperity, writing and performing spoken word poetry at her community's local bookstore, or curling up with a good book.

Michelle is passionate about transformational leadership, personal development, exceeding goals with a spirit of excellence, and keeping an open mind.

The topics of focus that are most important to Michelle are emotional intelligence, a growth mindset, and lifelong learning. Michelle believes these are necessary soft skills that are becoming increasing important in today's constantly changing global environment.

Michelle is available to speak to individuals and groups, as well as coach or mentor those who are ready to invest in and learn about themselves to go deeper into a growth mindset for prosperous results.

You may contact Michelle via:

Services: https://dornorconsulting.com/schedule-consultation

Products: https://linktr.ee/dornorconsulting

Booking: dornorconsulting@gmail.com

Website: www.dornorconsulting.com

Email: dornorconsulting@gmail.com

Buy Her Amazon Best Seller here! https://www.amazon.com/Pearls-Wisdom-Power-Spiritual-Advancement-ebook/dp/B0BR18TWRK/ref=tmm_kin_swatch_0?_encoding=UTF8&qid=1673285640&sr=1-1

OTHER BOOKS BY THE AUTHOR

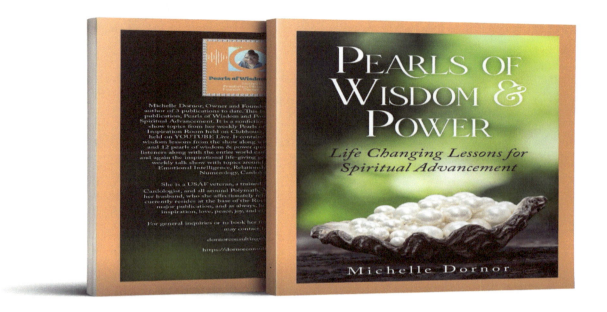

Pearls of Wisdom and Power: Life Changing Lessons for Spiritual Advancement

https://www.amazon.com/Pearls-Wisdom-Power-Spiritual-Advancement-ebook/dp/B0BR18TWRK/ref=tmm_kin_swatch_0?_encoding=UTF8&qid=1673285640&sr=1-1

A collection of 12 lessons from the Author's weekly podcast using esoteric knowledge such as Astrology, Numerology, Cardology and various spiritual literature to help you ascend on your spiritual journey. This nonfiction work is a collection of prior talk show topics from her weekly Pearls of Wisdom and Power Tuesday Inspiration Room held on Clubhouse, Wisdom App, and soon to be held on YOUTUBE Live. Faithful Listeners along with the entire world can read in written form again and again the spiritual gems Michelle often shares on her weekly talk show with topics around Mindset, Financial Literacy, Emotional Intelligence, Relationships, Spirituality, Astrology, Numerology, Cardology, and more.

Available at Amazon, Barnes & Noble, Apple Books, Target.com, Walmart.com and anywhere books are sold worldwide.

NETWORKING SUCCESS

The Blackness in Me: Lessons of Life from Cleveland to Accra

https://www.amazon.com/Blackness-Me-Poetic-Lessons-Cleveland-ebook/dp/B0B3RPTFNT/ref=sr_1_2?crid=2CYJF4E1R7TLC&keywords=Michelle+Dornor&qid=1673286505&sprefix=michelle+dornor%2Caps%2C139&sr=8-2

A moving collection of 23 pieces of intimate poetry about the author's personal experience while being Black in America and abroad. Written from the divine feminine perspective, it contains prose that will make you laugh, make you cry, and get you stirred to action. The celebration and history of Juneteenth was in mind as Michelle collected memories of her life as an adolescent to adulthood. There is something here for everyone to enjoy. With the stroke of her pen, Michelle weaves a wonderful tapestry of a collection that is heart wrenching at times, but also a beautiful journey through the lens of an African American woman in America who one day stepped foot on our ancestor's land in Accra, Ghana, West Africa.

Available on Amazon, Barnes & Noble, and anywhere books are sold worldwide.

She Her Hers: Inspiration for the Enlightened Woman's Soul

https://www.amazon.com/She-Her-Hers-Inspiration-Enlightened-ebook/dp/B0939YV318/ref=tmm_kin_swatch_0?_encoding=UTF8&qid=1673286505&sr=8-3

Her first major publication. It is a special Mother's Day 2021 edition. Designed for the spiritually awake woman from all walks of life. It contains 18 full length poems and prose to bliss the divine feminine within. Within, you will find musings about all the women and the roles they play. Her hope is that you will find inspiration, love, peace, and joy within these pages.

Available on Amazon in paperback or eBook.

Notes:

Notes: